Father Eugene O'Hagan, Father Martin O'Hagan and Father David Delargy attended St MacNissi's College, Garron Tower, and went on to study for the priesthood at St Joseph's Seminary, Belfast. They subsequently completed degrees in theology at the Pontifical Gregorian University in Rome while living at the Pontifical Irish College, and later completed postgraduate studies in the fields of Canon Law, Moral Theology and Education. Since then they have served in a variety of ministries as priests in the Diocese of Down and Connor.

D0814082

SOUL  SONG

Reflections on an Unexpected Journey

THE PRIESTS

Father David Delargy,
Father Eugene O'Hagan
and Father Martin O'Hagan

TRANSWORLD IRELAND

TRANSWORLD IRELAND
An imprint of The Random House Group Limited
20 Vauxhall Bridge Road, London SW1V 2SA
www.transworldbooks.co.uk

SOUL SONG
A TRANSWORLD IRELAND BOOK: 9781848271098

First published in 2010 by Transworld Ireland,
a division of Transworld Publishers
Transworld Ireland paperback edition published 2011

Addresses for Random House Group Ltd companies outside the UK
can be found at: www.randomhouse.co.uk
The Random House Group Ltd Reg. No. 954009

The Random House Group Limited supports the Forest Stewardship Council (FSC®), the
leading international forest-certification organisation. Our books carrying the FSC label are
printed on FSC®-certified paper. FSC is the only forest-certification scheme endorsed by the
leading environmental organisations, including Greenpeace. Our paper-procurement policy
can be found at www.randomhouse.co.uk/environment.

Typeset in Granjon by Falcon Oast Graphic Art Ltd.
Printed and bound by CPI Group (UK) Ltd, Croydon, CR0 4YY

2 4 6 8 10 9 7 5 3 1

For my parents, Francis and Colette, and
for my brother and sisters, with love.

Father David

We dedicate the thoughts and stories in this book
to our father, Francis, our brother and sisters,
and in memory of our mother, Joan,
who was a great influence in our lives.

Father Eugene and Father Martin

Let us begin this day with singing
whether we feel like it or not,
let us make glad sounds
and force our tongues to articulate
words of thanksgiving and praise.

Psalm 95

Contents

Soul Song

1

Beginnings

Whatever you do, or dream you can do,
begin it – boldness has genius, power and
magic in it. Begin it now.

Goethe

Father David

ROBERT MCMULLAN, MY MATERNAL grandfather, emigrated to New York in 1928, aged twenty-six. He went there as an economic migrant, just as countless Irish men and women had done before him and have done since, though in his case economic necessity was not the only, or even the principal, reason.

His father, Alexander, who had been in the Royal Irish Constabulary, thought it fitting that Robert should follow in his footsteps. So Robert was sent from his home in Glenariffe in County Antrim to the Phoenix Park in Dublin in order to receive the necessary training. Ireland in the 1920s was just emerging from a period of intense political and constitutional upheaval. Many nationalists in the northern six counties felt that constitutional issues were far from settled and there was still much to play for. Consequently there were some who looked none too kindly on a young man such as Robert joining the Royal Irish Constabulary, and who expressed this opinion to his parents in a manner which caused them to reconsider. It was to escape such pressures and potential dangers that young Robert abandoned his plans to join the Constabulary and turned his thoughts westwards to the opportunities that New York had to offer.

Mary McAuley, Robert's sweetheart, then aged twenty-one, was living in her parental home at Fallowvee, on the coast road below Carrivemurphy. It was a somewhat isolated spot in an area that was historically part of the summer estate of Lady Londonderry, close to Garron Point on the Antrim Coast. In front of and past their door wound the gloriously scenic coast road stretching from Larne to Ballycastle, which, between 1832 and 1842, had in a monumental feat of engineering been blasted out of the limestone rock. The construction of this road provided not only relief from unemployment for the local people in the days prior to the catastrophic potato famine, the great hunger of 1845–52, but also a military road into a previously inaccessible part of the country, which had been a refuge for insurgents during the 1798 rebellion.

Immediately behind the McAuley home and lapping the limestone and basalt rocks that constitute the Antrim coast lies the Sea of Moyle. This is the ancient and poetic name given to that part of the North Channel situated at the narrowest point between Ireland and the Mull of Kintyre in Scotland. From this point, on a clear day, there are magnificent views in an easterly direction towards Scotland and northwards across the bay to Cushendall, a picturesque market village sheltering at the foot of mighty Lurigethan.

Such a glorious, unspoilt, natural environment could not be more different from the towering skyscrapers, noise and hustle and bustle of the teeming modern metropolis that was New York, where in a few years' time Mary would find herself.

Before Robert left for New York, he and Mary reached an understanding that she would join him in America as soon as she could. He undertook to send some money home to help pay for her fare. True to his word, he wrote often, extolling the virtues of the wonderful, exciting place that was New York, whetting her appetite for the great adventure of coming to America, and sending her, in instalments, the fare that would permit her to join him, as they had agreed.

For Mary, however, given her pious upbringing and the social mores of the day, it would not have been seemly to go to Robert directly. As luck would have it, however, she had an aunt and some cousins already living in New York. They too had written to Mary, urging her to come across and offering her accommodation. So it was that on 17 May 1930, at the age of twenty-three, Mary McAuley boarded the SS *Caledonia* and set out from the Harland and Wolff docks in Belfast to make the long sea crossing that would take her to New York. As her ship passed along the coast she could make out her parents and her family standing at the back of the house – tiny black dots in the distance – waving her off with their white bed sheets.

On arrival in New York, Mary took up lodgings with her aunt and cousins in Brooklyn and set about making a living as a seamstress. She was thrilled to be reunited with Robert, but at the same time felt in no immediate hurry to wed. She relished the opportunities now available to her to socialize and make new friends. She loved to dance, and in New York there was no lack of opportunity. Inevitably she attracted new admirers, who, although she did not much encourage them, nevertheless posed an unwelcome challenge to Robert for her affections.

Robert, however, was a persistent suitor and on 28 June 1931 he and Mary were married at St Mary's Church in Long Island City, New York. Their first child, Robert, was born in May 1932. Almost immediately Mary found herself pregnant once again. The baby would be born the following summer. Realizing that the intense humidity of New York in the summer did not suit her, and overwhelmed with homesickness, she determined that this baby should be born in Ireland. Intending to take a holiday in Ireland and return to New York once the baby was born, with her husband's encouragement she and the boy Robert sailed home to Ireland, leaving Robert Senior to continue his work on the building sites in order to support his young and growing family.

Father David's grandparents, Robert and Mary, on their wedding day, 1931.

Back home in Ireland, in July of that year Mary gave birth to her second child, a girl whom she named Marese. By now, Mary was starting to have second thoughts about returning to New York. Exciting and exhilarating as that great city undoubtedly was, she did not consider it a suitable environment in which to bring up her young family. Her roots and indeed her heart were in Ireland, by the sea, where she had been born and had grown up. Furthermore, having been reunited with her family and friends in the Glens of Antrim, she could not bring herself to leave them all a second time.

She wrote to Robert in New York, suggesting that he should come home so they could rear their children in Ireland, which he duly did. They bought a dwelling at the church end of Red Bay, at the foot of Glenariffe, that glen known as the Queen of the Glens and arguably the most majestic of the nine scenic glens of Antrim. It was here, in a spot more or less equidistant from Mary's family at Fallowvee and Robert's in Foriff, that Robert and Mary settled down to rear their family of six – Robert, Marese, Colette (my mother), Dermot, Enda and baby Gerard (who died young) – and live out the rest of their days.

My grandparents' house was ideally situated to take advantage of the breathtakingly beautiful sea and mountain views. Looking out to sea, to the left was the small village of

Waterfoot, with its pier and the red arch making a passage for the coast road through the sandstone cliff, whose top was dominated by the ruins of Sir James McDonnell's castle, built in 1561 and the scene of many battles in the late sixteenth century. To the right was the white limestone arch which carried the railway to the old pier at Fallowvee. This was built to accommodate the boats that transported away the iron ore that was quarried in the mountain near Galboly. Further along the coast road was the White Lady, a chalk figure resembling a seated woman gazing out to sea, which had been formed over many centuries by the sea's erosion of the limestone rock.

Surrounding my grandparents' house was a garden, divided into four more or less equal parts. To the front, where the garden met the public road, was a well-trimmed lawn, used on warm summer evenings for playing bowls. Running parallel to the lawn were Mary's meticulously tended flowerbeds, displaying red, purple and pink fuchsias, golden honeysuckle and blue and pink hydrangeas, as well as wonderfully scented roses, dahlias, red hot pokers, daisies and many other flowers – all providing a riot of vivid colour in spring and summer.

Behind that, and largely hidden by the flowers, was a neat kitchen garden. That was Robert's domain, where, in order to provide for his growing family, he cultivated rows of potatoes, lettuce, cabbage, onions, leeks, carrots, turnips, spring onions, raspberries and gooseberries. The combination of fertile soil and Robert's careful tending resulted each year in a bumper harvest, and whenever my family or my cousins' families called to visit, we would invariably depart with a brown paper bag or a cardboard box packed with a variety of wonderfully fresh garden produce.

The section of the garden directly behind the house was shielded from public view. It was here that on warm summer days the babies and toddlers played, while the grown-ups sat around chatting and enjoying the afternoon sun. In one corner there was a rowing boat, complete with rowlocks, oars and fishing nets. In another corner there was a whitewashed shed roofed with weathered and rusted corrugated iron. Once upon a time it had been used as a byre – I recall looking on as a child in fascinated wonder as Robert and Uncle Dermot birthed a calf there – but mostly it seemed to me to be a mysterious dark cave, which, as one's eyes grew accustomed to the gloom, gradually revealed its contents to the curious: fishing rods, hooks and sinkers, assorted golf clubs, broken things, hurleys, old furniture, half-used paint tins, brightly striped canvas and wooden deck chairs, heavy, old-fashioned black push bikes, plant pots, assorted gardening implements, bags of fertilizer, coal and slack, and a stack of wood blocks and turf for the fire.

A low, white pebble-dashed wall, built by my grandfather, separated this part of the garden from a long red sandy beach. For us children, this was undoubtedly the main attraction. The sand, the sea, the waves and the rock pools provided us with limitless scope for exploration and fun – building sandcastles or damming the burn that flowed from Milltown under the road and across the beach to the sea, running races, playing rounders, kicking a ball, paddling as we made our way home with sweets from Peggy's shop, swimming, skimming flat rocks, boating, fishing for cod or mackerel, rock climbing, crabbing and shell hunting or bashing limpets off rocks – these were our summer seaside pastimes. There was always something entertaining to do and fun to be had.

For several years, my parents kept a good-sized caravan in a field beside my grandparents' house which easily accommodated my parents, my four sisters, my brother, our home help, Mary, our dog Rusty and me. To climb into our bunks each night, exhausted by the day's exertions, and be lulled to sleep by the crashing of the waves on the shore, or to awaken on a bright summer morning and hear the gentle lapping of the ebbing tide – these were magical experiences.

Father David as a schoolboy, aged five.

In the daytime, if it was wet outside, we might go across and play with our cousins in my grandparents' house or else stay in the caravan playing cards or reading, the caravan windows all misted up and running with condensation. But if it was dry and fine we stayed outside all day long, from early morning till late evening, with the beach and the sea as our limitless playground.

And on those days, or so it seemed to me, my grandmother, Mary, would always be there, standing at the low wall in the back garden, worriedly scanning the beach for sight of us, screening her eyes with her hand against the glare of the sun, and occasionally calling to us with an edge of anxiety in her voice if, in our fearless thirst for adventure, we had wandered too far up the beach or ventured out too far in the boat.

Father Martin

Journeys are by their nature full of surprises. They evoke a sense of adventure – and during the course of my life, music has guided me to many new horizons.

My mother was a significant influence on me right from

the start, as she was very musical – she was both a singer and a pianist – and so, inevitably, music and love are irrevocably entwined for me. A sense of rhythm and an appreciation of all types of music were instilled in me from my earliest days. Music expresses what is otherwise inexpressible; it is a language of the heart which reaches into the very inner depths of who we are.

Musical memory is a crucial element on the journey through life, as the mind gathers together pieces that have resonated over the years. Like a traveller revisiting favourite haunts, I return to these pieces again and again to be nourished and refreshed by them – as if falling upon an oasis in the desert.

My earliest musical memories date from my childhood in the country, a time of exploration and intrigue. If I wasn't digging for treasure like an archaeologist or sliding down the snowy driveway on my mother's tea tray in winter, I was being captivated by music.

I clearly remember the day when I heard one particular piece of music – from the big hit at the time, *The Sound of Music* – as it wafted through our house in Claudy, Hillcrest, Kinkull. The family was gathered around the piano: the two wee ones at the front, the older twins at the back and my brother Eugene in the middle. I recall rushing into what we called 'the good room' and shouting excitedly, 'Don't forget about me!' I was determined not to be left out because I loved those singing sessions, and the music that we created with my mother's help was magical. It seemed as if there was a fountain of music flowing in our home.

There was also the added delight of going somewhere to sing. My mother was a nurse and she would take us along to local nursing homes and to what was then the Waterside Hospital, where we loved to sing for the patients. There was a real feeling of connection with the patients and a sense of healing; the patients seemed soothed and delighted when they saw us tumbling in – my mother at the front and the Von Hagan family trooping in behind! Through experiences

The young O'Hagan family. Back row, from left: *Francis, father Frank, and Eugene.* Front row: *Joan, Martin, Martina and Mura.*

such as this I learned how music had the capacity to heal. It certainly played a pivotal role in our lives when my mother was herself ill in hospital, and later in my own life during times of stress.

Music continues to shape me in so many ways. Looking back to those early days, I realize there was a kind of electricity in the music we made, a blending that was instinctive. Perhaps it was also a meeting of mind and spirit, a form of unity which I found not only uplifting but empowering.

For example, I remember listening to a recording of Handel's music when I was seven or eight – during the 1970s, when our family was going through a period of change and upheaval. We were leaving our home in Claudy to live in Derry, and I'd found the record in a drawer that I was checking through just before we left the house. Almost immediately, I realized that I had discovered something rather special, a little piece of treasure. I put the record on the turntable and was instantly thrilled by the new sounds I was hearing.

My imagination went into overdrive and I was captivated by the sheer genius of the piece. The merging instruments, which I had never heard before, seemed to take me on a new path, and I knew with certainty that this was just the beginning of a wonderful new journey of discovery; I wanted to hear and experience more! There was a wonderful sense of symmetry about the piece, as if everything was orderly and made mathematical sense. I closed my eyes and pretended that I was boarding a boat that would take me down the River Thames, listening to the musicians in another boat as we journeyed down the river together. I was entranced by the sound of the violins dancing together, and it was to make a lasting impression on me.

During those days of black-and-white TV, we were encouraged to rely on our imagination for entertainment, and living in the countryside helped with this. We felt a real connection with the landscape, which was enhanced by our day-to-day activities: collecting basketfuls of berries, and then giving in to temptation and eating them all; dipping our toes in the river while waiting for our brothers and sisters to return home from school; playing in the snow and building snowmen in the mountains on icy winter days. This connection with nature was somehow linked to the music that surrounded me, and which seemed to flow with ease through each day, each experience.

Music had a spiritual dimension for me, too, for my mother played the organ in our parish church. I recall the atmosphere and the sense of mystery and delight that enveloped me as a child when I listened to the music filling every corner of that sacred space. It felt as if the music was seamlessly enhancing my developing faith.

The hymns and the solemnity of the church were replicated in play, as I pretended to celebrate Mass on a cardboard box in the living room, or held sacred processions in the garden with great pomp and ceremony. My brother Eugene took great delight in hearing our confessions – conducted in a wardrobe – although we never heard his!

All these experiences helped to shape me into the person I am today – and central to it all has been the love of music.

My parents both encouraged us all to sing and act, and my father, too, often took us to competitions or to concerts and hospitals to sing. My mother, who had been encouraged to sing by her parents, loved nothing more than to entertain, and she sang with great sensitivity and musical interpretation. Music had given her so much and she wanted to pass this gift on to us, by encouraging us and helping us to develop our singing talents as best we could. As a result, we all grew up with an awareness of the beauty and vitality of the human voice, an instrument that is an amazing gift from God. As we grew older, as we became used to singing at weddings, funerals and concerts and the stage became more familiar to us, we never took our gift for granted; this was something we simply enjoyed sharing with others.

Looking back, certain feelings and scenes from my childhood remain with me – such as the wave of emotion and belief which swept over me as I stood before the May altar, with beautiful spring violets and a statue of Our Lady resplendent upon it. I also remember music sessions at school, called 'singing together', which were overseen by our teacher, Mr McCourt, and were met with great enthusiasm. The memory of singing with great gusto at these sessions always brings a smile to my face. As I grew to appreciate the rhythm of the music, the words and the instruments, everything seemed to connect with me in a meaningful way, and being a member of the school choir and an altar server enhanced my faith and wonder at the sacred.

Clearly, my mind was being shaped by all these experiences, but it would be wrong of me to give the impression that everything was idyllic and carefree. We were, after all, living through some of the most terrible times, and the disjointed, deeply disturbed atmosphere in the City of Derry was palpable. Later, as a student and a priest, I came face to face with some sad, dark truths. Perhaps music played its part again in helping me and others escape from the horror of the Troubles. Against a background of pain, music nourished us both emotionally and spiritually.

Times were changing fast in the 1970s, and as my sisters

grew up and became more self-conscious, they decided against continuing to sing – except in the bathroom, of course! Modern bands and singers were helping to change the musical landscape and the likes of Abba and Michael Jackson were captivating our imagination and opening up a whole new world of pop music to us.

I clearly remember my first day at Garron Tower, the post-primary school, where I met a tiny nun called Sister Marie Gertrude. Small in stature but with a dynamic personality, Sister Marie Gertrude became a very influential figure in our lives, helping us to develop our voices and opening up new worlds for us. With her encouragement, my brother Eugene, my friend David and I sang in festivals, concerts, choirs and Gilbert and Sullivan operettas. Father McKavanah was another hugely influential teacher, and with his help we began to learn new roles, acting and singing in a series of operas. The hard work, endless rehearsals and camaraderie were fantastic, and the colour and excitement of the productions were a real eye-opener. We were in *The Pirates of Penzance*, *The Gondoliers*, *Savoyards*, *HMS Pinafore* and *Patience*, and as our voices began to change, one year we performed *Oliver Twist* and *Tom Sawyer*.

The discovery of this new musical genre was captivating

Gertie's boys: the influential music teacher Sister Marie Gertrude, with schoolboys Eugene, David and Martin, and the late Fr Raymond Fitzpatrick, who produced many school productions and gave great encouragement to all three young singers.

and added to our already rich tapestry of experiences. I believe that God in His Providence was at work, filling my life with music and the presence of the Divine, which has helped me through both the tough times and the joyful. Undoubtedly, there are times when I struggle with life, and I fumble around with the responsibilities and duties that fill my day. But music frees me and offers me a means by which to unravel life's complexities, and to cope with the hustle and bustle of the world in which I live. Music can also serve as a form of prayer, and I have relied on this so much in my life during the dark days, days that seem to hold no answers. At times like these I feel rootless and adrift, and it is often music that calls me back to that place where I can be still, where I can encounter the Divine. I thank God for all the musicians who have composed beautiful works of music across the centuries, who have brought their music to the world.

Every once in a while, you meet people who have the ability to change the course of your life, and I met such a person when I went to Queen's University, Belfast. Frank Capper was a music teacher, and stepping into his home was like stepping back in time. There was a sense of peace, serenity and calm about him, and his lessons opened up for me an entirely new treasure trove of magnificent music. I know now that he shaped and developed my voice in a way which, at just eighteen years old, I could not fully appreciate. He accompanied me with artistry and sang with a strong, brilliant voice.

Suddenly, I was hearing composers such as Delius, Vaughan Williams, Britten, Fauré and Finzi, among many others. Eugene, David and I began to sing at venues such as The Performers Club as our voices began to develop and mature, and we started to receive excellent feedback from our audiences.

I remember taking part in the oratorios performed in St Malachy's College as a clerical student in the early 1980s, and the sheer joy of taking part remains with me to this day. I am still lifted into a whole new world when I hear the sounds of

Haydn's Creation; the music draws me further and further into its heart and I feel truly blessed by its beauty.

> To you who read these lines of thought
> I address you.
> Step into the world that is mine, and yet
> not all mine but yours, if only you care to look.

Father Martin

Father Eugene

My brother Martin has recounted how our mother's musical background had a big influence on our lives, but looking back I know our father also played an important part in encouraging us down the musical path. His influence, however, was less direct than our mother's, because he was always so busy working as an official at the Ministry of Agriculture – more commonly known as a Potato Inspector. He always took great pride in his work and was well respected by his colleagues and all the local farmers.

When we were children, from time to time our mother

would play and sing for visitors who called at the house – a ceilidh, you might say, in the best of Irish traditions – and as we grew older I think she quickly realized that we could sing too. But the major catalyst for the five of us to sing together as a family – that is, my younger brother, Martin; me; and my sisters, Mura and Joan and Martina (our elder brother, Francis, never really got into singing) – was the release of *The Sound of Music*. We were captivated by the story of the Von Trapp family and their escape from Austria during the war. I think my mother must have got the idea that we could do something

Eugene on his First Holy Communion Day, 1966.

similar. So we began learning songs from *The Sound of Music* and from shows, as well as more contemporary pieces, like 'Boom Bang A Bang' by Lulu, which was very popular at the time. Once we had established our repertoire we took off, and I remember us singing at school concerts in our local village of Claudy, which is about ten miles outside Derry – which later became well known for the huge and terrible bomb that exploded there at the beginning of the Troubles.

I was also involved in music at primary school. I remember one concert when we were singing at the local intermediate school of St Patrick's and St Brigid's in Claudy, when one of the teachers asked me to conduct the choir. I was taken out of the choir to stand in front of what seemed to me to be a huge audience, and told to conduct. I remember feeling a bit self-conscious, and thinking that I would be much better singing in the choir than conducting it. However, I suppose they wanted somebody who they thought could carry it off, and that was my first solo performance. Since then, I've learned to turn around and face the audience.

One of the highlights of singing as a child involved us, the O'Hagan family, taking part in a talent competition in Cookstown, which is not all that far from Derry, but at the time seemed a huge distance away. I remember the excitement and the nerves as all six of us piled into the car with Mum and Dad and headed off. The heats went on week after week, and we got right through to the finals. As well as taking part in the family group, I also sang in the solo heats, performing 'Feed The Birds' from *Mary Poppins*, a lovely song which I still remember. As a family we ended up winning the competition – or at least our section of it – and as a soloist I came second to another young fellow.

After that we sang as a family group at various occasions. One I recall was for the opening of the Chimney Corner Hotel, outside Belfast. Belfast, of course, was going through a very bad time with the Troubles during the late sixties and early seventies, and the opening of this hotel was quite a big event because a lot of places were closing. Father Thomas O'Neill, a priest from the Cistercian Monastery at Portglenone, who was very friendly with our family and with a number of musicians and songwriters in the area, asked us to sing there. I remember it well because we enjoyed the thrill of being driven to the hotel by someone other than our father.

The event was compèred by the late Leo McCaffrey, who was a fine singer from Ballymena who had a band called Leo McCaffrey and the Glensmen. They had made various records which had done very well locally, and he was well known as a singer and as a compère. In fact, many years later, in July 1986, Leo McCaffrey compèred at my own ordination celebrations.

I suppose as children we had very few inhibitions and nerves; it was only later, as we got older, that Martin and I realized that this was fairly nerve-wracking stuff and that there was more to singing than simply keeping in tune. Our music teachers taught us to sing accurately and well, with feeling and with an understanding of the words, and we became increasingly aware of just how important a means of communication music and singing could be.

A significant event for me was leaving primary school to go to the 'big school'. I had, like many others, sat the eleven plus but failed it. I recall my father coming up to my bedroom to tell me the results. He read out the letter, which said that I was not suitable for a grammar-school education. I remember my father saying, 'That's not true,' and tearing the letter up and throwing it in the fire.

My elder brother, Francis, had also failed his eleven plus, but was now a boarder at St Columb's College in Derry, even though we lived only ten miles away. I realize now that that was the only way in which he could actually get in to St Columb's College, and that my mother and father had to make a significant financial sacrifice to send him there. He was very unhappy as a boarder, but was more than capable of coping with the academic education there, and I think my parents felt that the same would apply to me, although unlike Francis, who seemed to take learning very much in his stride, I always had to study harder.

I remember well going with my mother to an interview with the president of St Columb's College, who struck me as being a very serious, focused man, gracious in his welcome but nevertheless quite firm. I suspect he knew of my mother's reputation as a singer and was probably aware of our family's growing musical reputation in Derry and elsewhere. He pointed out candidly to my mother and to me that if I was to be admitted to the school I was expected to focus on academic subjects, and that as a result there was to be 'no music and no singing for this boy'.

It struck me at the time as an odd thing to say, but when you're looking to get into a grammar school, you go cap in hand. I think my parents were prepared to accept the restrictions that the president wanted to place on me in return for a place at the school. I am not blaming him. Many teachers and school principals at that time viewed music as something that ought to be pursued outside the academic curriculum, as a pastime or hobby. How things change!

Having secured a place at St Columb's College, much to my parents' relief, I spent the summer at home and at Portglenone Monastery. You might think that a strange place for a young fellow to go on holiday, but there were six children in our family, and we were not terribly wealthy.

At that stage, we were living in a large rented house about a mile outside the village of Claudy, where, as I have said, my father was the local Potato Inspector. There was no other income coming into the family apart from his wage, which although it wasn't wonderful was enough to keep the wolf from the door.

My mother and father, being fairly religious people, had become friendly with the Cistercian monks in Portglenone Monastery, and – probably to relieve the pressure of having the whole family at home during the summer holidays – the monks suggested that they would gladly take one of us for a little holiday. So I went there in August of that year, which would be 1971.

At that stage, the monks were building a new monastery, and during my time there (I was there for about a week or ten days in all) they gave me the job of picking up the little cement droppings that had fallen from the ceiling on to the floor of the new building, and removing them so that they could lay tiles on the floor. I thought that this was a hugely important job – indeed the construction of the whole monastery seemed to depend on me being able to identify these droplets of cement and rub them away with some sort of pumice stone.

I threw myself lock, stock and barrel into doing just that, and enjoyed my stay at the monastery immensely, all the more so because one of the priests there, Father Thomas O'Neill, was very interested in music. He had a little portable record player, which I thought was state-of-the-art technology, on which you could play small vinyl records – the 45rpm type. I remember there was a Dutch boy called Heinj who was very popular at the time, who sang songs like 'Two Little Stars', and I listened to those songs over and over and over again, in my little room in the monastery.

I wasn't aware of what the monks were doing. I knew that they were religious, but I wasn't involved in their celebrations. I was just there on holiday, and when I wasn't attending to those cement droppings I had a whale of a time visiting the forest nearby, paddling and swimming in the local river, and enjoying the kindness of the monks, who made me feel very welcome.

On one occasion during that holiday, a priest came down to the monastery to go to confession. There were a number of confessors at the monastery, and local priests would come for the Sacrament. Father O'Neill mentioned that I was a singer – and this priest turned out to be Father Patsy McKavanagh, himself a great musician. He readily accepted Father O'Neill's invitation to hear me sing.

From that moment, my life changed direction. Call it Fate, call it Providence, call it God's hand, but Father McKavanagh came into that room and he played the piano and we sang songs. I remember being amazed at his piano-playing. I think I sang 'Doe, A Deer' and 'Edelweiss' from *The Sound of Music*. He seemed impressed, and as he went up and down the piano, I sang scales. I didn't know where this priest was going to end on the piano, but I kept soaring up and up. I didn't realize I could go quite so high.

But anyway, that was that: the priest came, the priest heard me sing and the priest went away again.

Then he came back a second time, and we had lunch together in the refectory where the guests dined. I remember him asking me what school I was going to go to, and I told him that I was going to St Columb's College, Derry. He then asked if I had heard of Garron Tower, St MacNissi's College in County Antrim, near the coast at Carnlough, and I said no, I had never heard of it. He went on to explain that it was a school like St Columb's College and that people boarded there as well, and that they had a great musical tradition. Although I was interested, I think I was really too young to understand what Father McKavanagh was hinting at.

Finally it was time to return home, and my parents came to the monastery to collect me. This would have been the weekend before the start of the new school term. Father McKavanagh appeared again and spoke to my mother and father about sending me to Garron Tower instead of St Columb's College. When Father McKavanagh asked them to consider it, they asked me what I thought.

I would only have been eleven years old at the time, but I said I would be happy to go to Garron Tower. I can't remember exactly why I said this, but I think I was impressed by Father McKavanagh's kindness and also by the fact that it would give me a chance to do music, unlike St Columb's College.

There was the question of whether we could afford it, but Father McKavanagh insisted that lack of finances would not be a stumbling block and that we would work something out. I remember my mother in particular being a little sad that she was going to lose me to a school so far away.

It was different with my brother at St Columb's – it was only ten miles from home and my father often went in during the week to visit Francis, because he was so homesick there. He was going to stop boarding in his second year and I had been going to go to St Columb's as a day boy with him. But now I was going to Garron Tower as a boarder, which would change everything.

On that Sunday in September 1971 when my mother and father left me at Garron Tower, it was the first time I had ever seen the place. My first impression was that it was a huge, imposing building. It had been built as the summer residence of the Marchioness of Londonderry, but it had gone through many changes since her day – it had been burned down and restored, so what visitors now see is the facade of the original building, with a new building behind it to house dormitories and rooms for the students who board there.

I said goodbye to my parents and wept a few tears. However, my mother probably cried more than I did, because I was excited by the whole prospect, imagining it to be rather like a summer camp.

That impression, of course, changed quickly when the realities of boarding-school life kicked in. I had been put in the smallest of the dormitories, called Knockore, which was a bit run-down. I remember my mother and father being rather taken aback by its poor state of repair when we went to make my bed.

However, having said goodbye to my parents, I soon met up with some other new boys whom I befriended, and we explored our new environment and tried to get to grips with the geography of the place before getting to know the other boarders at the school.

I was probably no different from anybody else at school, but I was very conscious of being asked by my fellow students what football team I supported. I had absolutely no interest in football, but I pretended that I supported Man United in the hope that I would be accepted by the other Man United supporters. However, it soon became evident that I hadn't the first clue about football, the players or indeed the rules.

I went into 1C. There were two other classes ahead of me

– 1B and 1A. The C stream was for those who had failed their eleven plus or hadn't done so well. I remember my fellow students with affection – I think we all felt that we were in it together in that particular class.

During our first music lesson, the music teacher, Sister Marie Gertrude, auditioned each person in the class. We went in alphabetical order, so my name was well down the list. When it was eventually my turn, I remember her inviting me up to sing, and I sang 'Edelweiss'. When I had finished, everybody roared and cheered, and Sister Marie Gertrude then asked me to sing another song. I don't remember what I sang, but I do remember my classmates boasting to the other boys in 1B and 1A that we had a great singer in our class. I was greatly tickled by the whole thing and felt that if I couldn't play football, well at least I could sing.

That marked the beginning of a very long and happy friendship with Sister Marie Gertrude over the years at Garron Tower. From that day on things just got better and better, and my years at the school were the best years of my young life.

Garron Tower was renowned at that time for its performances of operettas in the Gilbert and Sullivan tradition, and because there were so many boarders there – nearly three hundred at one stage during my years there, between 1971 and 1978 – we were able to put on numerous productions, directed by Father McKavanagh and Sister Marie Gertrude. We all enjoyed these productions immensely in the winter months, and then in spring we had the music festivals in Belfast, Ballymena or Coleraine to look forward to. For the most part we went to Ballymena and Coleraine.

However, on one occasion we went to the Feis Ceol in Dublin, where I won the Boys' Solo. That was in the year before my voice broke. I was still eligible in terms of age for the Feis, but my voice was at that peculiar stage when it was just beginning to change. It was in a sense the crowning glory of my treble years at school to win such a prestigious prize, and the achievement was not lost upon the school or indeed the local press.

In addition to concerts and Gilbert and Sullivan perform-ances, as members of the school choir we also developed a keen interest in liturgical music. Again, Sister Marie Gertrude was central in teaching us this music: beautiful hymns, beautiful polyphony.

In many ways, the music that we sang in the college chapel provided us with a connection to the priests. The college was staffed by eight Diocesan priests as well as many lay people, and as boarders we came into contact with them on a daily basis, both inside and outside the classroom, and built up a friendly rapport with many of them.

Living in college enabled us to see the human side of these clergymen, and by being involved in making music in the college and taking part in all the regular duties and responsibilities of student life there, we became very familiar with the ways of the Church. Like many others in my year, I took it in turns to serve at Mass in the morning. The priests would come to celebrate individual Mass whilst Mass was going on in the college chapel for all the students.

My interest in the Church and the priesthood probably began even before I went to Garron Tower. I remember attending Mass as a young child with my parents, who were ordinary Catholic people, not in the least bit fanatical about their faith, but like other families brought us regularly to Mass each Sunday. I remember being curious about what the priest was doing up in the Sanctuary and around the altar.

Perhaps it was the theatricality of it all that fascinated me. There were the vestments, whose colours changed regularly, and then the priest was an old man who was probably quite eccentric in many ways. When I was old enough, like many of my friends at school I became an altar boy, and so I became au fait with the life of the local parish church. Much, of course, I didn't understand, but I found the choreography of the liturgy very attractive. And then there was the music, which seemed to go hand in hand with all that was happening. I would often attend these functions with my mother, since she played the organ, and I would join in the singing.

So music is mixed happily with my memories of childhood and early adolescence – taking part in liturgical celebrations in the life of the Church and of Garron Tower, getting to know the priests as human beings, and learning to see them not just as figures of authority or teachers, but more like benevolent uncles, who were there to help you when you needed help and to give you a little bit of encouragement and support.

In many respects, those of us who attended Garron Tower were very fortunate; we were very blessed to have had that experience and environment in which to grow up and be educated. That's not to say, of course, that it was a bed of roses all the time – that would not be true – but it was a place where I matured both musically and as an individual, through the encouragement and help of all the teachers, but especially of Sister Marie Gertrude and the priests.

In due course, the dreaded day arrived when it became evident that my voice was breaking. I think it was at the beginning of my third year, when I was due to take the part of Yum Yum in *The Mikado*. For some strange reason, whilst I was trying to learn the part, all of a sudden my voice, which had previously been able to reach the highest notes on the piano quite effortlessly, began to wobble and yodel, and I couldn't control it.

It caused me some embarrassment, it must be said, and for a long time Sister Marie Gertrude, who was teaching us, never said a word. But finally, when she and I were rehearsing on our own at the piano one day, she said, 'Eugene, I don't think you will be able to do the part of Yum Yum, because your voice is breaking.' I was so confused and sad in a sense, because I wanted to play Yum Yum. That might sound very childish – but acting was something I loved doing, and not to be able to do it came as a shock and a disappointment to me.

That day, one of the priests in the college came to find me in the music department, where I had been hiding all day, as I was so upset. He came up to the music room to console me and to talk to me about what was happening, because I had very little understanding of what was happening to my body, let alone to my voice. He was very kind and gentle with me as I cried my eyes out, but afterwards I was better able to accept it – albeit very, very reluctantly.

But it's funny how things happen in life, for that September or October, just when it had become painfully clear to me that my voice was breaking and that I couldn't take part in the college production that year, RTÉ suddenly announced that they were looking for a boy of about my age to audition for a part in a film of a short story called *Mr Sing My Heart's*

Delight, from Brian Friel's collection of stories *The Saucer of Larks*. I went for the audition – I can't remember where, it might have been Dublin – and I was given the role of the young boy in the story, which is told through the eyes of this young boy. So all of a sudden I was out of school and involved in something that was very, very exciting, a whole new experience for me. I had to go to Dublin, and there was a little rehearsal period in RTÉ's Donnybrook Studios, where I played along-side a lady called Doreen Hepburn and an actor from England called Mark Zuber – he was Mr Sing. We then went on loca-tion to County Donegal, up near Malin Head. Instead of staying with the rest of the production team in the local hotel, I stayed with a lovely family in the village for about a fortnight while we filmed. A lot of what happened went straight over my head, but it was a hugely exciting and challenging time.

I returned to school in late November or early December, and because I couldn't take part in *The Mikado* I became the accompanist's right-hand man and ended up turning the pages for Father McKavanagh, who was playing the piano in the orchestra pit.

Sister Marie Gertrude would normally have played the piano, but that year she was too sick to take part, even though she had spent long hours teaching all the students and putting them through their paces. So the bond that had already been created between us through music was strengthened, because although we both looked forward so much to these productions every year, this time neither of us was able to take part. I think the fact that we could share our disappointment made me feel a little bit better about it.

I am now going to fast-forward to the end of my time in school. I had moved up from the C stream into the A stream and ended up leaving Garron Tower with straight As in my three A-levels, which were English, Geography and History. At that point, I had to decide what I was going to study at university.

I applied to various universities, putting the local one, Queen's University, at the bottom of the list. You were always assured of getting an offer from the local university, so we were advised to put that last on the list as a safety net and see what offers would come in from other universities. I had applied to do law at these other universities, as I was interested in pursuing that as a possible career.

However, I applied to Queen's University to do a general Arts degree, because the thought was in my mind that maybe I should begin to explore the priesthood and see what it would be like to be a seminarian in the Diocese, and at the same time I could do my studies at Queen's University.

Before reaching this decision I had, like many of my class-mates, attended information weekends at the seminary, where we met the priests and students and got a sense of whether we would be interested in pursuing life in the seminary with a view to becoming a priest.

Finally, I decided that I would go to Queen's University and at the same time enter what we called the Wing – the seminary in the Diocese which provided students at Queen's with initial training as seminarians, before we completed our courses and went on to larger seminaries elsewhere. One reason why I decided to go to Queen's and the seminary in Belfast was that I felt that I would probably live to regret it if I didn't.

So I went up to Queen's University in Belfast in 1978, and I spent four very happy years there, although it must be said that they were very difficult years politically. It was a dangerous time – many people of my age were caught up in paramilitary activities which got them into deep trouble, and the college authorities – not to mention our parents – were painfully aware of the risks we faced walking around the security zone in the city centre, where you had to go through turnstiles and be searched by security officials before you could go into the shops.

Looking back on it now, it all seems quite bizarre and unreal. Everybody in Northern Ireland suffered as a result of the Troubles, because their quality of life was affected in many seen and unseen ways. But I suppose that way of life helped make us the people we are today.

Before leaving Garron Tower, I was fortunate enough to have the opportunity to be involved in a performance of Fauré's

Requiem that was being put on by a girls' school in Holywood, County Down. They needed a male voice to sing the part of the baritone, who performs the 'Libera Me, Domine' and some other parts of that wonderful work. The school, run by religious sisters, had approached Garron Tower for help, and Sister Gertrude proposed that I should go along and sing the part, because my voice had now deepened and settled. It hadn't, of course, developed, but it was sufficiently mature for me to be able to sing the baritone part. So I went along to this girls' school, where lots of the girls were interested in what I looked like and how I sang.

I remember meeting a girl there called Marie O'Sullivan, who I became very friendly with. She would write the odd letter to me just before I left Garron Tower, and when I went up to Queen's I arranged to meet her. She told me that she was going to a music teacher in Belfast called Frank Capper, and that he was one of the best teachers in the city.

So on Marie's recommendation, during my first semester at Queen's I approached Frank Capper for an audition, to see if I could learn to sing better with him. He asked me to come to his house, in the leafy part of South Belfast, with some music that I had prepared.

I remember the day very vividly. I went to his house, and was taken into a huge room full of antiques and a wonderful grand piano. Frank Capper himself was more like an Edwardian gentleman than a typical Belfast resident in the early eighties, and so I was quite intimidated by him. He spoke beautifully, with no apparent accent, and that impressed me too. And then he asked me to sing whilst he accompanied me.

At the end of the audition, he made me feel about half an inch tall by saying that the songs I had chosen to sing were for little girls. He also told me when I attempted to do some sight-reading that I was effectively musically illiterate.

Now I know I am not and never have been the greatest sight-reader, but that floored me, and I thought to myself, this man is supposed to be the greatest teacher in Belfast, but my goodness he is cruel. However, I realized that he knew what he was talking about and that if I wanted to learn anything this man would push me to the limit, and so I began to go to lessons with Frank Capper once a week.

Those first six months with Frank were the most demanding and frightening of my musical life. He was a firm taskmaster and made me work very hard, challenging me musically and giving me very difficult songs to learn. If I came in poorly prepared one week he would make it abundantly clear to me that if I was going to take music seriously I would have to work hard – harder than I was doing – and that this would inevitably involve sacrifice in terms of my social life, because I would have to practise regularly instead of going to the cinema, concerts and parties like other people of my age.

Although I found the self-discipline challenging in those first six months, I realized that I would be foolish not to stick at it, because Frank was indeed considered to be *the* best teacher in Belfast at the time. So I persevered, and after six months of him getting to know me and me getting to know him, we developed a strong friendship which deepened and matured over the years, and we remained firm friends right up until he died.

Frank was incredibly generous, because he realized that the £5 an hour he charged for lessons was a lot for me to find out of my student grant, and he only ever charged me for one official lesson per week, even though he often gave me two or maybe three extra lessons each week. He continued doing that throughout my four years at Queen's, preparing me for music festivals in Belfast and encouraging me to perform at the Performers' Club, a club which he directed and which was designed to give his students a platform upon which to practise their singing and their performance.

Martin and David, when they in their turn came to Queen's University and joined the seminary, also went to Frank Capper and experienced much the same challenges and encouragement that he had given me. They too performed at the Performers' Club, whose concerts were held twice a month in the Harty Room, in the music department at Queen's University.

We would all assemble there on a Sunday afternoon and Frank's pupils would take turns to present the music they had been working on. We did very demanding and challenging works by composers such as Hans Pfitzner and Benjamin

Britten, as well as traditional Irish ballads and pieces from various oratorios and operas. So we had a wide range of material, although we didn't actually choose the music ourselves – Frank selected the pieces he thought best suited each individual voice and then worked very hard on bringing us up to performance level.

I am happy to say that I did very well at the musical festivals I entered, winning numerous trophies and bursaries, which helped pay for my music lessons. I was fortunate to have the seminary's support for my musical activities, as indeed did Martin and David after me. The seminary authorities were normally quite strict about extra-curricular interests, but they were quite happy to allow me to take part in music festivals, and were especially pleased when I came home with a trophy or two.

So it worked out well for everybody. I got the opportunity to develop my music, and I contributed to the music in the seminary, leading the singing and practising with the other students once a week to prepare for various liturgies. I enjoyed that immensely and I think my fellow seminarians did too. I suspect the seminary authorities were quietly proud that one of their students was doing so well in the world of music in Belfast.

In a sense, through the music he taught, Frank Capper shielded us from all that was happening politically and in society in general at that time. Music allowed us to lift our hearts and extend our horizons beyond the limits imposed on us by the very difficult circumstances of the times.

2

Gifts

You give but little when you give of your possessions.
It is when you give of yourself that you truly give.

Kahlil Gibran

Father Martin

I RECENTLY WENT TO TWO EVENTS where I was somehow transported to a different world. The first was a concert by a pianist who had written two pieces of music, one called 'Yellow' and the other called 'Orange'. When the music began the whole atmosphere in the concert hall changed; instead of the usual gentle bustle, there seemed to be a sudden feeling of tranquillity and peace. I felt as if the music had invaded my mind and spoken to my soul. I was very impressed by the musician's obvious musical gifts and the ease with which she shared her talents and communicated with the audience.

The second event was also a musical performance, but this time by a violinist, who played with such intensity that I felt quite overwhelmed; the music once again drew me into another world and I felt both soothed and refreshed by it. I was reminded that music brings the past into the present; gifted composers from years gone by live on through their music, whilst contemporary composers create exciting new pieces for today and tomorrow.

It is important to recognize that we all have gifts and talents, and that they shape not only ourselves, but those around us, when we embrace them and share them. Sometimes, however, we fail to recognize our gifts, perhaps because we have never been encouraged to do so.

For example, when I visit schools, children will speak about how good they might be at sport, reading or writing, and this is all very admirable. But when I ask who is the kindest, the most gentle or the most sensitive among them, it's not a question they have necessarily considered before. Suddenly they seem to realize that gifts are not all about achievements – other attributes are just as valid and valuable. If we can view things from this perspective, we can engage with the world in a new and perhaps more enlightened way.

I often think of the gifted people who have enabled so many others to grow in stature, those who have changed the world for the better. There are the massively influential figures such as Gandhi, Nelson Mandela and the late Archbishop Oscar Romero, for example, men whose insight and sheer conviction led to great changes in the world; these men have quite simply opened up new opportunities for millions of people. But it is important to recognize that the innate gifts that lie within us all, and which have been shaped by our life experiences, can nourish and support others in many different ways.

We don't have to hit the headlines or change entire countries to make a significant contribution to others.

I remember watching a film about a sculptor talking about her family as they were digging for turf. With them was a young girl who was given a piece of clay to play with while the rest of the family busied themselves with their digging. With that simple act, as the child formed the clay into shapes with her tiny hands, a wellspring of creativity was born. That little girl later grew into a young woman who has dedicated her life to sculpture and art; through her creativity, she is able to share her talents, and offer inspiration to others.

Sometimes, it isn't until we find ourselves in difficult circumstances, when we are stretched to the limit, that we recognize that we have certain gifts. Although at the time we may not fully appreciate our resourcefulness, or our ability to withstand pressures or overcome problems, these challenges can be the most fruitful and most empowering opportunities. Through these experiences, we may discover a new strength, a new identity and sense of purpose. Indeed, when we are called to dig deep, to be resilient, not to give up, perhaps then we discover our true selves and the gifts that have lain dormant within us.

I have had the privilege of seeing how the power of a particular gift can shape a family, and how, in the face of difficulties, such a gift can help to forge a strong bond that is able to withstand the most testing of times. Building a strong and resourceful family unit is an incredible challenge in today's world, when there are so many distractions and seemingly attractive opportunities outside the home. At the heart of a family – be it the traditional family, a group of friends who love and support one another, or a teacher who encourages the endeavours of his pupils – there is an unconditional love that spurs us on to achieve all that we are able to.

Some families, of course, live in very difficult circumstances and not everyone is lucky enough to be part of a warm and nurturing family. I remember being in Rwanda in the early nineties with the charity Trocaire, and I will never forget what I saw. I was stunned at how people could be so cruel to each other, and appalled at the devastation that surrounded me. I tried to make sense of the confusion and the pain that blighted people's lives. And yet, even in this dark place, there was hope. I visited a village where we were told that a mother had given birth to a child, and I remember going to meet and congratulate the young woman and to ask if there was anything that she needed. In the midst of all the chaos, I will never forget her reaction; this young woman was so full of joy, and she felt so blessed to have a visit from a stranger. I felt completely humbled by her response and her gift for sharing her happiness with me. This encounter had an enduring effect on me, and this young mother's gentleness and resilience gave me real hope that Rwanda had a future – that this land, torn apart by misery, was going to bear fruit. I hope and pray that the baby born that day is now making his way in the world, and helping others in his homeland.

The modern world continues to move forward, and we should take time to recognize that progress often comes about because ordinary people – unsung heroes – are making a real, tangible contribution to society. Think for a moment about the foster parents who give a home, and a real chance of a new life, to a vulnerable child; the teacher who sows the seeds of knowledge in a young pupil, who then goes on to journey well in the world; the artist who inspires us and adds those essential colours to the palette of our lives. I have always been impressed by the artist Michelangelo. I marvel at his work, which stirs in me so many emotions. I wonder at the perfection of the statue of David, and relish its simplicity.

Whatever it is that inspires and sustains us – art, poetry, music, the sciences, our faith, our prayers – it is important to recognize that when we are inspired, we bring out the best in ourselves. If we are fortunate enough to have educational opportunities that develop our talents, we can reach more confidently for new possibilities and new adventures. We can blossom. For education is as much about gaining inspiration

Father Martin (third from left) in the Irish College Choir, Rome, 1988.

and learning how to interact with others as it is about passing exams or achieving academic qualifications.

In my own life, I must acknowledge the vital influence of my parents, whose love and sense of sacrifice undoubtedly shaped me into who I am today. As a family, we may not have had a great deal materially, but we grew up in a happy, nurturing environment where each child's talents and gifts were recognized and encouraged. How fortunate we were.

I think of the simple gifts that surrounded me, the youngest in the family. As we lived in the countryside, the landscape forged in me a love of nature and inspired me. For example, I remember lying on the bank of the river that flowed near our house on a hot summer's day, noticing how the sun danced on the surface of the gently rippling water. Beside me was a box of gooseberries, the result of our efforts that morning. I was the custodian of the box while the rest of the family paddled further upstream. (I recall eating all the fruit and waiting anxiously for their response when they rejoined me!) On days like this I definitely felt a sense of connection with the world around me, and I am forever thankful to God for allowing me to experience nature, and to have the time to notice, to reflect, to question the world during the course of my childhood. I also recall with gratitude the gentle discipline with which my parents raised us, the boundaries they set and the direction they gave us. And all the time there was the gift of music.

As I mentioned in the first chapter, the concerts my family gave were so much fun, and so uplifting, that I grew to understand that music had a transformative power that could lift the spirit and lighten the darkest days. Visiting hospitals with my family and singing for patients was a great example of the healing power of music, and what a wonderful gift it was to give to others. Even as a young child, I was learning through music how to relate to those who were in need of comfort.

These early memories serve not only to remind me of happy days, and the rough and tumble of family life, but remind me that my parents truly were a wonderful gift from God. Although we were not sheltered from the harsh political realities of the world around us, we were encouraged to use our imagination and were not in any way pressurized, like so many young people are today, to strive incessantly for academic qualifications. In our very competitive society, achievements – be they at school, on the sports field or in the workplace – count for a great deal; this can often lead to disappointment and failure, which can be difficult to handle.

I believe that the imagination is a significant and much neglected wellspring of creativity – a wonderful source of hope and inspiration – and I know it has helped to make me the person that I am today. As a result of this wellspring, I feel that I am tuned in to all of life's emotional ripples – the ebb and flow that encourages us to experience and learn new things. In terms of faith, I believe that imagination can open new avenues of thought, for creativity is a gift from God. We only have to look around us to see the gifts of creation – gifts which encourage us to live every moment to the full, to capture each experience and learn from it.

Music has opened so many doors for me and I know it has been a fantastic gift from God. Music has allowed me to abandon my self-imposed limitations, to cross the boundaries that can sometimes exist in life, and it has undoubtedly played a crucial part in my life; it is a gift that enables me to grow, to give and to receive with gratitude.

When I reflect on my journey through life, I realize that God has always been beside me, equipping me for the various challenges that I have faced. I can now see that I was being shown, firsthand, through the example set by my parents, how a depth of faith could shape me and prepare me for my vocation to the priesthood. Others, too, have been hugely influential, people such as Sister Marie Gertrude and Father McKavanagh, who were such pivotal figures during my schooldays.

The sheer enjoyment of people coming together in harmony can bring joy and colour into the dark shadowlands that can sometimes engulf us. So it is important to look into ourselves, seek out whatever gift or talent we possess, and try to share it with others. For in sharing our gifts, we also receive.

Lord, help me in my need.
Banish my fears,
Increase my faith.
Hold me in Your love
And fill me with Your peace.

A short prayer learned by my father, Frank Senior, as a child

Father Eugene

I'm often approached by people looking for records that will help them compile their family tree. Parish records are a rich source of information, containing references to times, places and, most important of all, people. We are all fascinated by our ancestry and where we come from, and we place great store on what we can learn about our past, because it tells us something about who we are. Old pictures revealing quirky family features – the shape of a nose, the curve of an eyebrow – never cease to interest us. To some extent, who we are is passed on to us through our genes, but to think that we are merely a product of the genetic mixture we inherit would be too simple an explanation of the mystery of life.

We are all truly unique. Each of us is a one-off. We may have a lot in common, but there is so much that sets us apart, and that's the fun and challenge of being a human being, made, to quote from the Old Testament, in 'the image and likeness of God'. Each of us is a gift to the world and to each other. If we could only remember that and have it affirmed by others every day, there would be much less anger, envy, jealousy and pride in our world. Wouldn't that be a gift?

Father Eugene out and about on his parish duties.

We all carry within us the potential to make a difference in the world and to many peoples' lives. In essence, we each have a gift. It may not be obvious to the world at large – indeed, your gift may not even be obvious to you. Sometimes it's hard to believe we have anything to offer, which is almost as bad as believing we have everything to offer, that we have gifts or talents that we really do not possess. In today's society, sometimes it can be easy to have the impression that anyone can become a star or celebrity, regardless of talent. Once the wheels of the music or film industry begin moving, people believe that anything is possible – that the sky's the limit. The downside of this, of course, is that many people, especially the young and inexperienced, believe that stars are created overnight, and that if they don't succeed in becoming the celebrity they crave to be, and receive the adulation of the public, they will never be happy, contented and fulfilled.

Difficult though it may be to admit, this kind of fulfilment is ephemeral and disappears as quickly as the morning mist; it brings little long-term satisfaction or happiness. No, the type of gift I'm thinking about is the one that may never receive the acknowledgement that it truly deserves. The kindness of a nurse or carer in a hospital, the hand of a stranger that reaches out to steady you as you stumble – gifts of compassion and support given in times of need. These gifts will rarely be widely recognized – but do you stop being kind, gentle, hopeful, encouraging, loving, patient, inspiring, or a true friend, simply because it's never reported in the papers, on TV or on the internet?

These are the kind of gifts that can make a lasting difference to your life, and should never be taken for granted. You may never win an Oscar, but you are still that fantastic actor who brings a world to life on stage; you may never win a Brit Award, but you are still an authentic performer who brings joy to others; you may never be Teacher of the Year or Nurse of the Year, but you still inspire young minds to go on searching for knowledge and wisdom, or restore your patients to health. These are the gifts that money cannot buy, and if you are able to share your gifts with others, they can make a huge difference to the world.

We give and receive gifts at various times of the year – birthdays, Mother's Day, weddings – but I suppose the main time of year for exchanging gifts is Christmas. However, gift-giving is just one way in which we can show our gratitude, love and appreciation for those we care about.

In the Christian tradition – the tradition I know best – the Magi (the Three Wise Men in Matthew's Gospel) set off on a long journey and eventually arrived in Bethlehem to visit the newborn baby Jesus. They came from somewhere in the East – we're not entirely sure where – and followed a moving star, which finally led them to their journey's end: the humble stable.

The men had taken a great risk in setting out from their homeland in search of the newborn king; they risked being duped by Herod. Whether you view the story with scepticism or with belief, what strikes me most is that these three men went on a journey into a strange and unknown land, and into a strange and unknown future, but they had confidence and the resolve to see that journey through because they were determined to welcome the new baby – the baby whose birth was a magnificent gift to the world. That sort of outlook never fails to encourage the rest of us, whenever we feel a little unsure of where we should be going and what we should be doing with our lives.

The Wise Men, identified as Caspar, Melchior and Balthazar, didn't travel empty-handed. They carried gifts of gold, frankincense and myrrh – one gift each. These gifts were a precious cargo for them and no doubt they packed them carefully for the long journey ahead. But there came a time when those gifts were unpacked and revealed – and each was handed over for a particular use.

We're told that gold was given to the baby Jesus in recognition of his position as king; frankincense was a sign of his godliness, and myrrh – the ointment used for embalming bodies – foretold his untimely death. These were not the kind of gifts one would normally give to a child, but their significance is not lost on us. Today, when we celebrate Christmas by giving gifts to families, friends and loved ones, we continue the tradition of that great celebration that began so many centuries ago.

Life is a long journey, and at times we're not sure where we're going or where that journey might end. Like the Wise Men, we carry precious gifts with us, but unlike the Wise Men, who were able to read the signs of Jesus's birth and followed a star to find him, we often need others to help us on our journey, and to help us recognize and unpack the gifts we have wrapped up within us. Those who help us can be our families, our friends, our teachers – they are the ones who believe in us and who can inspire us. They are the ones who do not count the cost, who go the extra mile. Without their tireless encouragement and support, we might never realize our gifts. Undoubtedly, there are times when we need to be pushed, otherwise we could all too easily settle for the easiest option and fail to fulfil our potential. That would be a pity, because our gifts would remain in their boxes, unopened, unused.

There's that wonderful parable Jesus told of the master who went abroad and gave his servants five talents, three talents and one talent respectively, according to each one's ability (Matthew 25, 14–30). The talent in the parable was a sum of money, but it could easily stand for the gifts God gives us. The men who received more than one talent went and made more, but the man who received only one talent 'went off and dug a hole in the ground and hid his master's money'. Upon his return, the master was less than happy with the man who had hidden his talent in the ground and done nothing with it. It was taken away from him and given to the man who already had more. This is a powerful parable and could easily be applied to you or me, as it encourages us to use whatever gifts we have been given. As Jesus said, 'No one lights a lamp and puts it in a hiding place or under a basket, but on a lampstand, so that those who enter may see its light.' (Luke 11: 33) That's what your gift is. It is a light for others to see and to see by. So let your light shine.

Father David

Ever since August 2002, when the then bishop of Down and Connor, Patrick Walsh, asked me to take up the administration of the parish of Whitehouse, it has been my custom to spend half an hour or so before the Vigil Mass on a Saturday evening and again before Mass on Sunday morning in personal prayer before the Blessed Sacrament. It's a habit I have retained since coming to the parish of Hannahstown in August 2006, where by the grace of God and the will of the bishop I am, at the time of writing, the incumbent parish priest.

I have never found it easy to pray. I am too easily distracted. I wish it were otherwise. Prayer takes discipline. Putting in place a timetable of regular prayer is, I find, a great support in maintaining what in my case might generously be termed a 'prayer life'.

Eucharistic adoration, that is, prayer before the Blessed Sacrament exposed in the monstrance upon the altar, helps me prepare both mentally and spiritually for the celebration of Mass. Certain types of music, I have found, can be a great aid to stilling the heart and mind and helping to direct the human spirit heavenward. Arvo Pärt's 'Alina' has for some time been serving that purpose for me in Hannahstown.

Clearly, others have learned to appreciate the benefits to be gained from meditating before the Blessed Sacrament, and, over time, some parishioners and visitors from other parishes have started to come along early to church to join in a time of quiet prayer. That half-hour before Mass is a special time. Even in the relative stillness, with each person engaged in his or her own thoughts, there is a powerful sense of connectedness and solidarity – God's people, come before Him in prayer.

One Saturday evening, as I was giving the benediction with the monstrance, I noticed a couple of new faces in the congregation. Visitors. A good-looking, fair-haired woman and a tall, professional-looking man. I was curious. Who were they? After Mass, as I stood on the church steps greeting the departing congregation, they came along and introduced themselves as Andrew and Roisin, from the Clonard area of Belfast. Roisin is a reader at Mass in Clonard Monastery, and when not fulfilling that extraordinary ministry they like to come to Hannahstown on account of the Eucharistic adoration.

Roisin explained that she and Andrew had recently returned from a year working among street children and the poor in Pattaya in Thailand. A television crew had accompanied them at various stages throughout that year and a documentary programme telling their story, intriguingly titled *A Year in Sin City*, was to be broadcast the following evening. Maybe if I wasn't busy I might like to watch it, they suggested.

At that time, a TV crew had recently been following me to make a documentary about The Priests, from the signing of our recording contract with Sony on the steps of Westminster Cathedral in April 2008 through to the performance of our first public concert, in September of that same year, in the wonderful St Patrick's Cathedral in Armagh. I was interested to meet others who had also been the subject of a TV documentary and I was curious to learn more about their story.

To all appearances, Andrew and Roisin were an ordinary, middle-aged, middle-class couple. But it soon became apparent that, at least in some respects, they were far from ordinary. Roisin was the manager of a busy dental practice in Belfast and Andrew was a teacher, and they had cared for their aged parents for some years, up until their deaths.

After Roisin's father – the last of their parents – died, they felt themselves to be at something of a loose end. A sense of purposelessness had started to develop – an emptiness crying out to be filled. And then one evening, Roisin turned to Andrew and said, 'Why don't we just sell up, get rid of all our stuff and go and see more of the world?'

To make a radical break – to take a year out from their jobs, sell their house, get rid of all their accumulated and unnecessary possessions – to do something interesting, like spending a year travelling in Europe in their motorhome, then come home and write a book about pilgrimage sites in Europe – that initial idea may have been Roisin's. But Andrew readily agreed, to Roisin's great surprise, and he was happy to collaborate.

Of course, it was all a bit spontaneous and not at all well thought out, and in the end, apart from the bit about selling their house and giving away all their accumulated worldly goods, things didn't really work out at all as Roisin had initially imagined. But the conversation that evening generated a shared enthusiasm to do something different and interesting and exciting. It planted a seed in their minds that would germinate, and in due course would blossom into a series of life-changing experiences that would affect not only Andrew and Roisin, but countless others in a way that Andrew and Roisin could never have foreseen.

A priest friend, on learning of their plan to bring their motorhome to Europe, suggested a different course of action. 'It's probably not a great idea to rush into such a major decision,' he said. 'Obviously you are going through something of a transitional experience in your lives. The Marianella Centre in Dublin is running a three-month course for people in transition. It's a sabbatical course aimed specifically at missionary priests and nuns, but you would probably benefit a lot from it too. Why don't you try to get on that course and then see how you feel? There's no rush. You can decide afterwards what you want to do.'

And so it was that Andrew and Roisin sold their house, gave away all their surplus possessions and set off for Dublin. Three months later, refreshed spiritually by the seminars and inspired by the experiences recounted by the forty-four missioners on the course, they now had to make a major decision. Where to next? As Roisin explains, 'We had changed and matured over three months, and having met these amazing people from all over the globe, we realized that ordinary people were the force for change and for good in the world, and somehow we wanted to use our talents and do something for others less fortunate.' In that spirit, Roisin and Andrew set off for Thailand to work for a year at the Redemptorist-run orphanage in Pattaya.

In recent years, Pattaya has acquired an unsavoury reputation as a locus for sex tourism. At one time, it was a simple fishing village in an unspoilt, idyllic location – an ideal spot for exhausted American soldiers needing respite from the madness that was the Vietnam war. Think crystal-clear blue sea, palm-fringed, white sandy beaches, and gentle, friendly locals with a ready smile on their lips and a heart for hospitality. That was what Pattaya was like before the war. Very quickly, however, prostitution became a feature of life there, and by the time the soldiers had gone home and tourists had come along to take their place, the sex industry was well and truly established.

Nowadays there is a thriving tourism industry, with five-star luxury resorts sitting cheek by jowl with great poverty and deprivation. Poor people from the country come to the city looking for regular employment and find none. Such a set of circumstances facilitates the sexual exploitation not only of women, but also of young men and children. Survival often comes at a high price.

Coming from a relatively affluent Western society with Christian values and culture, nothing could have prepared Andrew and Roisin for what they would experience in Pattaya. Those early days were undoubtedly difficult and challenging. Andrew, in particular, struggled to cope with the overt sex tourism that is such a feature of life in downtown Pattaya. Consequently, for that first year he confined himself by and large to the area around the Redemptorist House, where he found an outlet for his talents in web design.

Roisin began helping out at the Redemptorist-run orphanage, but as there was already a surplus of volunteers and assistants working there, she soon felt under-utilized and unfulfilled. When she expressed her dissatisfaction, it was suggested that she might prefer to work with abandoned street children and the poor families living around the city. And so Roisin found herself working each day alongside a young Thai woman called Khun Noi, who became her guide, interpreter, co-worker and great friend.

As Roisin describes, 'I started going out into the streets with my new Thai friend, Khun Noi, where we met many young street children, hungry and willing to do anything for a foreigner in exchange for a few baht or some food. These kids were prey for the human traffickers and paedophiles, who were drawn to this Thai city where anything could be bought for a small price.

'Slowly gaining their confidence and eventually going into the slums where they lived, I spent most of my time talking to and listening to their families, who were practically invisible to the rich tourists and an embarrassment to their government, and who had no sense of dignity or self-belief. I wept and thought, someone has to do something!'

But after three months, it all started to get too much for Roisin. A combination of the heat, the poverty and the enormous extent and complexity of the problems she encountered began to affect her. She and Andrew were thousands of miles from home. They had no great financial resources and were unable to speak the language. They felt powerless to do anything worthwhile. They questioned God, governments, human nature and even themselves.

Feeling down and disheartened, they began to consider throwing in the towel and going home. But a phone call to their priest friend back in Ireland led to a change of heart. 'Don't think you have to change it all,' he said. 'Just do what you can. Take just one person you can make a difference to and concentrate on them.' And that's what they did.

About six months after they had first come to Pattaya, one day Andrew and Roisin were visiting some poor families when they met a poor woman clearly in a very distressed state. Due to a deformity of her palate, the woman had difficulty speaking, but through Khun Noi they learned her name: Khun Au.

Khun Au and her husband had come to Pattaya from the border near Cambodia to find work. The chief cause of her distress was the fact that her husband had died just the previous evening. As if that were not bad enough, just two days earlier, two drunken Thai men had come into her house and raped her in front of her dying husband. By the time Roisin and Andrew found her she was in a terrible state – distraught, grief-stricken, helpless, vulnerable and terrified. They tried to comfort her as best they could.

But they could see that as well as needing the love and sympathy they were only too willing to give, she also needed practical help. Her home was an old shop that had been

Khun Au with Roisin in Pattaya.

partially destroyed, with walls on only three sides, so the one-room building was open to the curious gaze of every passer-by and to the elements. There was no privacy and, crucially, no security. What Khun Au needed most was a place to live that would at least be safe and secure.

It took some time for Andrew and Roisin to gain Khun Au's trust, but within a few weeks they were able to help her move to a new home – a modest one-room structure, but most importantly, one with a door, a lock and a key.

Over the next few months, Andrew and Roisin spent lots of time in Khun Au's company. Khun Noi, their collaborator and friend, was often there too, acting as interpreter. But words weren't always necessary. More often than not, all that was needed was a smiling face, a hug, a holding of hands, gentle and comforting tones. Khun Au gradually came to know that she was loved and cared for. She was not alone in this world. She was not worthless. Because Andrew and Roisin believed in her, she slowly began to believe in herself, and in her human worth and dignity. In the warmth of Andrew and Roisin's care, she thrived, and in time she was able to get her life together and resume her work of gathering for recycling the discarded plastic bottles that littered the streets of Pattaya.

But there was to be a further serious setback for Khun Au. Some time later, she suffered a stroke. She was found lying in the street and was brought to hospital, but she was sent home with nothing more than paracetamol – the cheap and convenient cure-all for those with no financial means. Roisin and Andrew paid for Khun Au to be brought to Bangkok Pattaya Hospital, where she received proper medical care and intensive physiotherapy, as a result of which she made a good recovery.

Eventually, Roisin and Andrew's year in Pattaya came to an end. As they packed their bags and prepared to leave for the airport in Bangkok, they did not feel any great sense of achievement. Certainly, there had been some successes along the way, Khun Au being one of them. But when all was said and done, they had only been scratching the surface of the problem.

The problems and difficulties in Pattaya were just too great. Nothing had really changed. It hadn't turned out to be the rewarding, life-changing experience they had hoped for and anticipated. They were left with a real feeling of emptiness and a sense of failure. They felt flat.

All that week, their good friend Khun Noi had been very quiet and withdrawn. She was upset that Roisin and Andrew were leaving and she couldn't bring herself to speak about it. But now she phoned them and asked them to come out of their small room to say goodbye.

They were met by a sight for sore eyes. All the families from the slums they had worked with during the past year had gathered to bid them farewell. They had prepared garlands and spent what few baht they had on presents. They were crying and seemed genuinely upset that Andrew and Roisin were leaving. They said that the pair had changed their lives completely: their love for them and their belief in them as God's children had given them hope, and they wanted to thank them.

It was a deeply moving experience. As Roisin puts it, 'Twelve months of feeling useless and frustrated, twelve months of thinking someone should do something, twelve months of sitting quietly day after day with people who had been abandoned by their own society, and wanting so much to help but not knowing how . . . and then they told us that twelve months of love and care for their plight and the knowledge that they were not alone had given them strength. I suddenly remembered the words of Gandhi – "Be the change you want to see in the world" – and I realized how right he was.'

During those twelve months in Pattaya, Roisin and Andrew had given so much of themselves, and the expression of gratitude they received on the last day was an eloquent and moving testimony to how much that gift was appreciated.

But the giving was by no means all in one direction.

Certainly, in the beginning, Roisin and Andrew had been genuinely moved by the hardship, suffering and poverty they witnessed. And within their limited means and resources they acted in a compassionate way to do something practical to help. It was undoubtedly a source of deep joy for them to see Khun Au doing so well. That, and the unexpected expression of love and thanks on their last day by the families they had helped, reinforced the message that in spite of the enormous scale of the poverty and need that exists in the world, it is still possible for ordinary men and women, in small and simple ways, to make a real difference. It was for this that they had come to Thailand: to have such experiences and to learn such life-changing lessons.

On returning to Ireland, as Andrew and Roisin reflected on their Thailand adventure, everything looked different. Their experiences provided them with the inspiration and impetus to found a charitable trust, Kate's Project, named after

Roisin's late mother. Now, with the support of friends, family and many others, Kate's Project is providing practical help to many families in the slum areas of Pattaya.

Realizing that education is a crucial factor in helping people to escape the cycle of poverty, Kate's Project helps illiterate parents and grandparents complete the legal registration documentation that will enable their children to attend government-run schools. By providing school uniforms, shoes, books, school meals and fees, the charity enables 150 children to receive an education. Abandoned children living at risk on the streets are offered a safe refuge in a community along with other children, where they receive an education and care for one another.

In January 2009, Roisin and Andrew opened an office in Pattaya and called it Kate's Project – Centre of Hope, and that is what it is, a place where individuals and families without hope can come to find it. As the promotional leaflet states, it is a centre where people are made to feel welcome, where they can learn crafts, get seeds and learn to grow their own food and sell the extra in the markets. It is a place where people know someone cares; that someone loves them and believes in them.

There has since been good news regarding Khun Au. Her daughter, whom Khun Au had not seen since she and her husband moved away to find work, learned that she was alive and living in Pattaya. She came four hundred miles to find her mother and persuaded her to come and live with her and the three grandchildren she didn't even know she had. Khun Au is now reunited with her family and living very happily.

It's a story with a happy ending, but it would not have been possible without the compassionate hearts and the generosity of Andrew and Roisin.

The gap that was left in Roisin and Andrew's lives after the deaths of their parents has been filled with the new families they have acquired in Pattaya. They have received a new and fulfilling purpose in life. Andrew has given up his job as a teacher and now earns a living as a freelance web designer. Roisin works part-time as housekeeper to the parish priest of Hannahstown, a task for which she is clearly over-qualified, but which suits her perfectly as it allows her the flexibility to devote her free time to running Kate's Project from home. She is in daily contact with her good friend Khun Noi and a new assistant, Anan, and through them with her Thai families. She and Andrew visit the project regularly throughout the year.

Recently a friend of mine, after praising me for using what she termed my 'God-given' gifts, went on to make the following observation: 'If you were to put your gifts on a set of scales and measure them against the gifts of others, they would all weigh exactly the same. There would be a perfect balance.' What my friend wanted me to understand was that, while we have all received different gifts, they each have the same weight and value in God's eyes. It's what we do with them that really counts.

3

Life's Lessons

*Life is a succession of lessons which must
be lived to be understood.*

Ralph Waldo Emerson

Father Martin

JOURNEYING CAN INVOLVE A REAL sense of purpose, of savouring every moment – and reflecting on our experiences can help to shape and mould us as we learn from our triumphs and our disasters. Reflecting on our journey can also help us to make sense of our life.

Growing up in an emerging technological world – that was not quite as frenetic as the world we live in today – allowed me more face-to-face communication with friends and family than is usual nowadays, and although this was enriching, it was not without its difficulties.

Being the youngest in the family, I felt a real sense of protection as a child, and I recall many of my childhood experiences as life-giving moments. These experiences ranged from joining my father as he travelled to work, to playing with my brothers and sisters – and having the space and freedom to run around in our home in the countryside.

On reflection, the lesson I learned at the time – to savour

the pleasures presented to me – was a significant one, which has remained with me into adulthood. I have happy memories of simple family pleasures – the outdoor life, picnics in the countryside, building snowmen, enjoying the delights of freshly baked bread at a neighbour's house. And perhaps this ability to look back with great fondness on those early days has helped me to appreciate not only my past, but my present.

But life wasn't always fun. From an early age, I was aware of my mother being very ill and I was grateful to God for her recovery. She was a very special woman and the sacrifices she and my father made for the family played a crucial part in our journey to adulthood.

Over the years, I have also learned the importance of friendship. At the age of eleven, when I ventured away from the familiar setting of home to begin my new school, there was a real sense that I was leaving a warm and secure haven – a place of love and laughter. I admit that I felt quite a bit of anxiety about leaving, for I was embarking on a journey into another world – I was about to become a little fish in a much bigger pond. However, as is the case for most children, these phases marked new growth and a host of new opportunities.

But if school opened up new horizons, the days that followed were marked by darkness, which descended upon the region when the Troubles erupted in Northern Ireland. Horrendous violence seemed to take place on a daily basis, and stories of death and destruction permeated the community like a plague. So much sadness and so much grief.

I learned to value the everyday normality that we all take for granted now, for in those days we were forced into a kind of survival mode. There was no sense of normality or freedom, just a deadening feeling of coping as best we could – and being powerless to change things for the better. We were never sure what was going to happen next. Derry certainly was a solemn, sombre place then, and when my family moved to the city in the early 1970s, I recall that there was always a heaviness in the air. And yet, buoyed up by music, family and friends, we all continued our journey through life, crossing the bridges built by those who had particular courage. Watching how others managed to be optimistic in the face of adversity helped me to keep going.

Life, as they say, goes on, and I could see myself growing and changing. I longed for everything around me to be just right. Perhaps this search for perfection emanates from feelings of inadequacy and is something that others feel too when, like me, they struggle with the fact that we have to accept ourselves for what we are – warts and all. But the life lessons we experience help to challenge us, and mould us into something new. With God's help, we emerge from each of life's challenges not broken but stronger and more resilient.

When we are inspired or encouraged by others, we sow the seeds of faith and begin to form new and exciting pictures, like a beautiful mosaic. With the help of others, we can leave behind loneliness and isolation. I know from my own experience that the most important lessons I have learned in life have been taught me by others.

When I went to Queen's University, a new world opened up. Without the daily routines and structure of school life, I became very aware of the responsibilities on my shoulders. As I studied hard and journeyed ever closer to the priesthood, this new and exciting world left a strong impression on me and I relished the chance it gave me to grow. I was exposed to a wider slice of life, which enabled me to savour so much more and which raised so many questions – such as who are we, and what is our purpose here on earth?

It was, of course, a difficult time because we were in the thick of the Troubles; there was a real sense of paralysis and helplessness. I recall clinging to a wall as police frisked a young man in front of me and found a gun; watching a bus being hijacked and burned. This is the dark side of living in a violent society – a society which longed for normality. Most people simply wanted the little things that make up everyday life to return. So the lessons I learned at this time involved coping with the violence that surrounded me, meeting people from other faiths in search of common ground, enjoying our shared experience of music, being challenged – and all the while, hoping that a solution could be found to alleviate the misery around me.

It is hard to remember all the lessons that I've learned on my journey through life, but I think it is important to reflect on life's experiences and the situations that have challenged us. Being taken out of our comfort zone can stretch us and can lead to new horizons. For example, when I was heading to Rome to study, I encountered not only a new language but a new culture and I had to draw on all the resources I could – including the Church, the lessons I had learned at school, my family and my

Father Martin meeting Pope John Paul II after the Good Friday Ceremony in St Peter's Basilica, Rome, 1989.

friends – to give me the courage to learn and grow in this very different environment. But I was fortunate to have the love and support I needed, and I think it is vital that we never underestimate the impact friends and all those who shape us can have on our lives. Rome proved to be a wonderful, life-affirming experience. Despite the hard work, I managed to have fun, and gained so much from this incredible opportunity.

Perhaps in discussing life's lessons, we should also focus on how important it is to try to inject warmth, humour and fun into our everyday life. Humour lifts our spirits – even when we laugh at ourselves! Laughter can be a friendly companion that travels with us on our journey through life, and I thank God that despite some difficult times, I have always tried to find the lighter, less depressing side of life.

As a parish priest, I work with communities whose faith and trust is challenged almost every day. Loneliness, ill health, economic problems – and, of course, the terrible violence that has touched so many of the people I serve – this is all part of everyday life. And whether I'm visiting the sick, encountering the young shoots of faith in children and young adults, journeying with couples as they approach marriage, or even attending the scene of a murder, I place myself in God's hands and seek His guidance to help me. Sometimes I question and doubt; sometimes waves of anxiety overwhelm me. But this is, I realize, all part of the work I have been called to do – and I learn important lessons from it almost every day.

Music has given me so many chances to escape into another world and has opened so many doors for me. I am forever grateful to God for this, and to all those who have given me the encouragement and support to progress over the years. Music is the language of the heart and soul, and the voice is the only instrument that is an innate part of a human being. But you don't have to be able to sing to enjoy music, or to use it to escape from the rigours of life. The resonating power of music enables us all to have moments of connection, and helps make sense of life's undercurrents and the problems we all face. Music heals the soul, and I like to think that God can speak to us through this incredible medium.

The past few years have been something of a balancing act for me, where I have had to juggle my commitments. But I believe that nothing happens without a reason, and I am conscious of a sense of providence in all that we are doing. Grasping the moment and taking the opportunity to bring joy to others is an enormous privilege, and one I don't take lightly. Everyday concerns preoccupy me, of course, but music enables me to face daily challenges and intensifies my relationship with God.

God has been the cornerstone to all my life experiences. He shapes us and provides opportunities for us to grasp. I pray I will always have the tenacity and courage to do justice to God's glory and to the work I feel called to do. I have learned to savour life, to reflect, to grasp the moment, and to face the ever-changing landscape of society with all its strengths and weaknesses, accepting the brokenness in my own life. And in all this, faith is the matrix, the key, the starting point.

> Journey with us in the threads of life
> and weave the pattern of hope
> into our hearts.
> In the hustle of life, the strains and stresses
> grant us your peace and enable us to
> follow You Lord with calm.

Father Martin

Father Eugene

As the years pass by, each birthday offers an opportunity to reflect on life. Having just turned fifty, I can't avoid asking what have I learned about myself, other people and the world, as well as the big questions such as why am I here, what am I doing and where am I going?

In thinking about the lessons I've learned over the years, I recall the words of Saint Paul, who said, 'When I was a child, I talked like a child, I thought like a child, I reasoned like a child. When I became a man, I put childish ways behind me.' (1 Corinthians 13:11) Saint Paul's words provide me with a helpful starting point from which to reflect back. New experiences, of course, are not restricted to one's childhood or early years. Life continually offers all kinds of unexpected events, meetings, friendships, joys and sorrows; that's what makes it so interesting and challenging – and sometimes wonderful.

My brother Martin and I are blessed in having a father who is in his nineties. He is a fount of information about the 'old days' and as he gets older he talks more frequently about his boyhood, and about his relationship with his granddad, his father (who died relatively young), his siblings and his mother. Not all his experiences were happy ones and the times in which he lived were very different from my own times as a child and adult. But like my father, I am ultimately the product of my past – or, at least, heavily influenced by it – and perhaps that's why I have always been fascinated to find out about our family's roots.

We should remember, however, that we are not absolutely determined by our DNA and what we have inherited from the family. We may have no control over the colour of our hair – unless, of course, we help nature a little bit – but we are more than the sum of our molecules and cells. Each one of us is unique – a one-off never to be repeated. That makes each of us special.

As I have already related, when I was eleven years old I failed the dreaded eleven-plus exam, and my father threw the letter announcing that I was 'not suitable for grammar-school education' in the fire. His reaction and his confidence in my abilities made the world of difference to me. I was lucky. After that, providence dictated that I would go to school at Garron Tower, where, a couple of years later, Martin joined me. Looking back now, I realize how lucky I was to have the opportunity to attend this school; I met people whom I still count as good friends today, and with whom I share many happy memories.

In effect, I grew up at Garron Tower. I went there as a twelve-year-old boy and left at eighteen – a young man on the threshold of life. During those years I matured both mentally and physically, and my relationship with my siblings and parents developed and changed too. To be truthful, our relationship was not always harmonious, but thankfully, it was never so confrontational as to undermine the love that was always there.

Growing up in an all-boys' school has undoubtedly left its mark on me, as I'm sure it has on others. Notwithstanding the protective environment of the school, as boy boarders each of us had to learn certain survival skills; it was a fairly challenging environment and we were expected to be self-reliant, punctual, studious, courteous, well-mannered, respectful and diligent. I now appreciate that these virtues and values, which present a daily challenge to this day, make life more pleasant and life-affirming, both for ourselves and for others.

But what about the darker side of growing up – the little disappointments, jealousies, fears, sibling rivalry, broken friendships and trusts betrayed? These were all part of learning about life, learning to take responsibility for the things we say or don't say, the things we do or don't do.

I love to travel, and my first experience of travelling independently was when I was eighteen and planned a trip to London with a school friend. I'd led a fairly sheltered life and my parents were, understandably, a little anxious. But I'd just finished my A-levels and was on the brink of going to university, if my results were good enough, and my friend and I felt we were old and wise enough to head off on our own. I still remember that first trip 'abroad'. London was a very different world to the one we had experienced until then, and the sense of freedom and adventure – which is still part of every trip or holiday I take – was very special. They say travel broadens the mind, and that, in my experience, is certainly true. No matter where I go, I love to find out about the place and its people. I was lucky enough to spend seven years studying in Rome, which has given me a real love for that city and many aspects of the Italian way of life.

Whenever I have been away, I have returned home with slightly changed ideas or attitudes about the town, country, or people I have just visited. I might also return having learned something more about myself. Although the increased security at airports and ports, the delays and the drudgery of getting to and from a holiday or a work commitment can sometimes make travelling a gruelling experience, in my book it's always worth the effort, just to broaden my horizons.

I enjoy meeting new people, having the opportunity to savour another culture and way of life. Such experiences add to the richness and diversity of life, and can make the routines we live with a little bit easier to embrace on a cold, wet and wintry morning. So I never take these opportunities for granted, and try to learn from each and every one of them.

Looking back to my school days, I see how the eight years I spent in Belfast and particularly the years I spent in Rome taught me the value of teamwork. In the latter years of study for the priesthood in Rome, I found myself in the company of some wonderful fellow students from all over Ireland and elsewhere. We had all been thrown together, and had landed in the Irish College in Rome, where, with a little study and God's grace, we would eventually serve. Being in a relatively small college, we had to work together and were expected to take responsibility for all sorts of everyday practicalities. Whilst a healthy independence was never discouraged, and team effort was never highlighted as a 'must do', I think we soon realized the value of working as a team on various levels. That was sometimes a real challenge, especially when someone, myself included, thought they knew better. It is hard not to be right all the time! But teamwork was an important lesson to learn – and one that proved invaluable when, years later, Martin, David and I began to work together as The Priests.

In the course of my life, I've learned that the ability to collaborate in all sorts of circumstances, and with various individuals and groups, is a necessity rather than a luxury – and it's particularly important in my role as a parish priest.

In my early days of priesthood, I don't mind admitting that I could rightly have been described as an impatient young man. A newly ordained priest is like a new recruit to any company; they see many of the good things the company has to offer, but they also see the bad things too. They are keen to make changes, to implement their innovative ideas as soon as

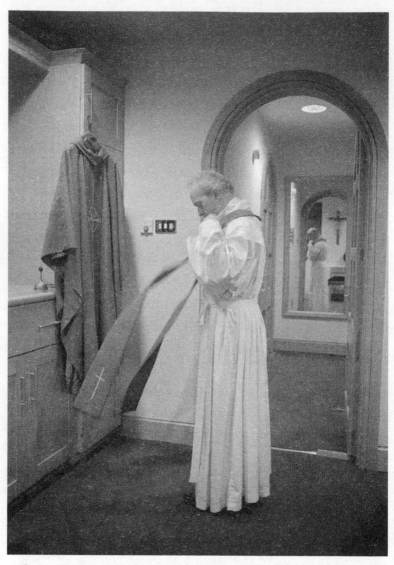

Father Eugene getting ready for Mass in Sacred Heart sacristy, Ballyclare.

possible. As a fresh young priest, I recognized the great strengths and appeal of the Church, but I also felt a little frustrated that the things I had studied, and which really enthused me while I was still studying for the priesthood, were not evident on the ground when I came home to serve in the Diocese and my first parish.

Of course, with the benefit of hindsight, I now know there was much happening on the ground that I did not value highly enough – but being a young and impetuous newly ordained priest, I thought I had all the answers. I still have my dreams for the Church and for the role that I may be able to play in it, but experience has taught me not to undervalue or underestimate the great goodwill and dedicated work, much of it voluntary, which already exists and has done so for many years.

Despite the inevitable imperfections that afflict the institution that is the Church, the selfless dedication of so many people around me, both clerical and lay, has encouraged me to keep working: the small charity group in my parish; the wonderful teachers at the small local school; the faithful who come regularly to Mass, and those who don't; my colleagues in the Tribunal. All these hardworking people have been, and continue to be, a great support and inspiration to me – the embodiment of teamwork in action. Over the years, I've learned to be patient about the life and practice of the Church, and to be tolerant towards those people whose criticisms – justified or unjustified – would at one time have caused me to respond in haste and make a difficult situation much worse. I try to be patient when things don't go the way I would like them to go – that is to say, my way! Perhaps one of the biggest lessons I've learned is to accept the help and care of others. I'm working on it, but appreciate I still have a long way to go, and know that I'm just a little too self-reliant for my own good!

There's an old saying: acquaintances are many, but friends are few. I still meet up with one or two friends from my school days, and although these meetings may be infrequent, when we do get together it feels like slipping a hand into a well-worn glove. There's a sense of relaxing, of being able to be oneself in another's company without any pretence and without being on one's guard.

Other friends have included our music teachers, especially the late Sister Marie Gertrude and the late Frank Capper. Both were wonderful people from very contrasting backgrounds, the former from a strong faith base and the latter from a Christian background too, but with more than a hint of agnosticism. Music linked us all together, and my relationship with them developed gradually from one of respect – which should always exist between a pupil and a teacher – to a deep and lasting friendship of many years.

Gertie guided me through the more confusing and traumatic experiences of growing up at school, and coached me through that difficult vocal transition from being a treble to a tenor. She was a welcome female presence in a predominantly male environment, and she was a mentor and friend right up until the day she died at the age of ninety-three. It was a privilege for David, Martin and me to sing at her funeral and to say our goodbyes, until we meet again.

Frank Capper was an altogether different personality. A gentleman, a pianist, a vocal tutor, he was, as I have said before, a demanding teacher, but a true inspiration and friend. His knowledge of the vocal repertoire was immense and his collection of vocal scores unparalleled. It was he who really taught me the value of commitment. Frank didn't suffer fools gladly and was quite intolerant of anyone who didn't take music lessons seriously, often advising them to consider taking up knitting as an alternative! Although initially I thought his approach was a little harsh, as I got to know Frank better I came to appreciate his love of and dedication to music, and he inspired me to take it seriously and to make music an important part of my life, because he felt I had a talent worth developing. But he warned that it would take time, effort and commitment. This was a wonderful lesson, and I make a point of encouraging others to persevere, to develop their talents whenever possible, because they will yield a rich harvest.

The mistakes we make in life should, if we take the time to reflect, teach us important lessons. We all make mistakes of one kind or another, and we all have our regrets. Not to learn from them would be a disaster. And yet, when I've said to myself 'I'll never do that again!', almost inevitably, at some later date, I have once again fallen into the same old trap and I wonder if I have learned anything at all. But to quote Alexander Pope, 'to err is human, to forgive divine' – and I guess we all deserve a second chance. If we genuinely try to learn from our mistakes, and help others to overcome their difficulties, we can only benefit ourselves and others. With the guidance of the religious tradition to which I belong, a healthy balance can be found in the Sacred Scriptures between failure and forgiveness, disappointment and hope.

One of the best examples of the triumph of love and forgiveness over ingratitude and selfishness must be the parable of the Prodigal Son. The unbounded love of God, represented by the father in the parable, overrides his son's self-obsession and restores a balance to his life that gives the son the chance to recapture his humanity. There is the possibility of a second chance, after all.

Generosity and hospitality are prized elements in the ancient Rule of Saint Benedict. These qualities are given pride of place in the daily life of all Benedictine monks, and their practical expression can be seen in the kindness shown to the stranger, the visitor, the traveller.

I have experienced this hospitality countless times on my travels as a penniless student and am eternally grateful for the generosity shown me over the years, a generosity which I still experience at the hands of my friends, parishioners and closest colleagues. It is a quality I've learned to nurture in my own life and in my dealings with other people.

At times, it hasn't been easy, especially when it comes to making myself available. Giving one's time is a different kind of generosity from being generous with money, which can be relatively easy to do. Being generous when it comes to spending time with another person can be a real challenge and a real blessing.

It seems as if we are all in a race against time these days; we have schedules to keep, deadlines to meet, reports to complete, tasks to fulfil, calls to make, bills to pay. There is never enough time for other people or for oneself in this increasingly frenetic world in which we live. There is even less time for God in our lives, which is a pity, when you consider that He has made time for us out of eternity.

Father David

Over the years I have spent working as a priest in various parishes, I have been privileged to meet and get to know some truly wonderful human beings. Many of them have since passed on to their eternal reward. As I remember some of them now and reflect on their lives, I recall some of the ways in which their lives touched mine and I appreciate anew what a rich source of inspiration they have been to me in my own life.

Many of the most valuable lessons that I have learned in life have come from these individuals, who I'm sure had not the slightest idea of the effect they had on me. Would that I were more like them, for I confess that while I regard their many fine qualities with admiration, I often fail to apply those lessons personally. But then, I am still on my pilgrimage and perhaps God in His mercy will give me time. I am happy to share a few of their stories with you, dear reader, in the hope that you too might be lifted up by them as I have been and may find a little nourishment for your soul.

Harry's Story

Harry McCluskey was a remarkable man. In fact, he was one of the most interesting and fascinating characters I have ever met. One of the many duties of a priest in parish ministry is to visit the sick and bring communion to those who are housebound and unable to come to church. According to custom, these visits are conducted on the first Friday of each month. So it was on the first Friday in September 1997, just a few weeks after I started as the new curate in the parish of Glenavy and Killead, that I came to visit Harry at his home in Crumlin. That was the start of my fascination with Harry.

It was his garden that struck me first. It was a small plot of only a few square metres, but, oh, what a glorious garden! It stood out from all the neighbouring gardens by virtue of the fact that it was a riot of vivid colour, with a profusion of scented flowers crammed into that small space. The reason for such an overwhelming abundance of flora soon became apparent as one by one, in a continuous and steady stream, bees began to arrive, as if to escort me on my walk up the garden path to the front door. Like aeroplanes circling in a queue and waiting to land on a busy airport runway, the bees buzzed and hovered and queued up to land on a miniature wooden ramp that was attached to the front door. Then, one by one, they crawled through a small hole and down a clear tube into a beehive that sat just inside the porch. Harry kept a beehive *inside* his house and feasted on a diet of fresh honey every day.

At ninety-seven, he was a great advertisement for the benefits of such a diet. Thin as a reed, he looked and spoke and moved like a man nearly twenty years his junior. When I complimented him on this remarkable fact, as if to demonstrate the truth of it he suddenly sprang out of his chair like a jack-in-the-box, stretched both arms up to the ceiling before swooping down to touch his toes, and then straightened up tall again with arms akimbo and a triumphant expression on his face, as if to say, 'Well . . . what do you think of that?' It really was impressive.

The walls of Harry's compact sitting room were almost entirely covered with a multitude of clocks of every shape and size. Some of these Harry had made himself, while others, which belonged to friends and neighbours, were in various stages of repair. There were several antique grandfather clocks with their swinging pendulums and innumerable smaller wall-mounted clocks. Cuckoo clocks were Harry's particular favourite, and there was even one that chimed every quarter-hour with a different type of bird call. So as we chatted, our conversation was punctuated with an incessant ticking and tocking, whirring and chiming, whistling and cheeping and the calls of a whole asylum of cuckoos.

Harry McCluskey was unlike anyone I had ever met before, and I was captivated. After that first visit, whenever I went on my rounds on the first Friday of each month, I

Harry McCluskey.

would deliberately leave him to the last just so that I could spend a little more time in his company, and listen to his reminiscences.

I learned that as a young man, Harry cycled from Crumlin to Bangor for work every day for five years – a round trip of sixty miles over some quite steep terrain. There were no light-weight aluminium frames or multi-speed gears in those days. His was one of those old-fashioned, heavy black bikes with a broad saddle you sat upright on, whose only luxury was a bell and maybe a basket. When I asked him why he had gone to such trouble, he explained that employment was scarce and it was worth making an effort to hold on to a good job, even though it entailed hardship and great inconvenience.

It's hard to imagine a young person of my own or subsequent generations putting up with such a punishing regime. It is a completely different world that we live in today and unfortunately we take so much of our comfortable modern lives for granted. Nowadays we expect not to have to wait for things. We want things now, a.s.a.p. — preferably yesterday, if the truth be told. Should the object of our desire be withheld or our plans be thwarted for even a short time, we become upset. Impatience leads to foul temper and road rage. And when we obtain the thing we desire, we may enjoy it for a while, but if it becomes broken or damaged or if another newer and better model becomes available, the thing we felt we couldn't live without is cast aside or thrown out. So much about our modern world is instant and disposable.

Harry, on the other hand, was a man of immense patience. Perhaps it came from his being a keen fisherman, willing and happy to spend long hours fly-fishing in Crumlin Glen. Harry knew how to wait. Not for him the easy-come, easy-go attitude or the quick fix. He was a craftsman. The things he crafted with his own hands took months of painstaking work: a grandfather clock — its wood grain smoothed and hand-polished over time with a canvas rag; a standard lamp, its wood twisted into a spiral by honeysuckle years in the growing, and its lampshade painstakingly wrought from hand-picked rushes. Harry could turn his hand to almost anything. In the garden he could make pears grow from a plum tree, and many a salmon came from the local river, tempted by the flies that Harry crafted.

Harry's long life spanned the twentieth century. In the course of that life he had witnessed so many changes, from horse-drawn carts to cars, and from planes to space rockets and man landing on the moon. So many changes and, alas, not all of them for the good. Harry lamented the damage done to the environment and to people's health by pesticides and chemical pollution. He was scandalized by what he saw as a decline in standards of behaviour among many people today and their lack of respect for almost everything.

And maybe that was the very thing that was at the heart of the man. Harry had a profound respect for everything in the world around him. He had respect for himself and for other people. He had respect for nature and wildlife, for the environment, for a piece of wood, for an insect, for the soil.

The things that interested Harry, the things he knew so much about, are by and large a mystery to people of my generation and younger. So caught up are we in the fast pace of modern life, entranced and distracted by gizmos and gadgets, technology and virtual reality, that we have to a great extent lost touch with the real world of nature that surrounds us. So many of us no longer take time to notice, never mind smell, the flowers, and it seems to me that our lives are so much poorer and stunted because of that.

In the book of Genesis, we read that God made man and set him over creation, to be master of the fish of the sea and the birds of the air, to tend the earth and grow plants. Harry was a good and faithful steward of creation. And just as he was in touch with the seasons and the soil, so also he was in touch with the Master Craftsman who created it all. And everything that was His he approached in humility and with great reverence. There was so much about Harry that was in the image and likeness of God – so much that was good. Like a branch firmly attached to the vine, he never failed to produce good fruit in his life and in his friendships. I thank God for having known him and for the example he gave of a human life lived well and with dignity.

Teresa's Story

After Easter in April 1998, I had gone away on holiday and it was only on my return that I heard the shocking news that there had been a murder in the parish. Ciaran Heffron was just twenty-two years old. He was 'a quiet and likeable lad', according to Father Brian Mullan, the chaplain at the University of Ulster in Coleraine where Ciaran was a student. He had returned home that weekend to visit his mother, Teresa, who was ill with cancer and was due to go into hospital the following week. On the evening of Friday 24 April, Ciaran had gone out to a local pub, the Fiddler's Inn, for a drink with friends. Later, in the early hours of Saturday morning as he made his way home alone on foot, he was abducted by loyalist gunmen and shot several times in the head, and his body was dumped by the side of the road near the bus depot.

When his father, Hugh, realized that Ciaran had not yet returned to the family home, he set out on foot to look for him. As he approached the village, he became aware of a commotion up ahead – police cars, an ambulance, flashing lights – and saw that part of the street had been cordoned off with tape. After making enquiries, he was informed that there had been an incident; a young man had been shot dead. When Hugh explained to the police officer that he was out looking for his son who had not returned home earlier that evening as expected, he was invited to take a look. That was how Hugh came to identify the body of his own son, Northern Ireland's latest sectarian murder victim.

Had I not been away on holiday at the time, it would have fallen to me to minister to the family and conduct the funeral, for the Heffrons lived at my end of the parish. But this wasn't a normal death and there wasn't only the family to consider, for Ciaran's murder had left the whole community shocked and deeply traumatized. Community relations in Crumlin at that time were fragile, to say the least. There was very deep resentment brewing among many nationalist and republican residents over what they viewed as sectarian parades by the Orange Order and 'kick the Pope'-type pipe bands through the village. It was possible that for some hotheads, Ciaran's murder might have been the last straw. People were speculating about who was responsible for the murder, and the names of some local troublemakers were already being openly mentioned. There was immense, raw anger in the air and the desire for retaliation was palpable.

As if the situation were not complicated enough already, TV camera crews and newspaper reporters had gathered in the village and Ciaran's funeral was to be conducted in the full glare of the media spotlight. I know that as a relatively inexperienced curate I would have found the whole situation immensely difficult. Privately, I felt hugely relieved to find on my return that Father John O'Sullivan, the parish priest, had conducted the funeral.

At Ciaran's funeral in Mater Dei Church in Crumlin, Father O'Sullivan addressed hundreds of mourners from both sides of the community, saying, 'Some time on Friday evening, some evil men decided that a Catholic young man should die in Crumlin. The only reason for his killing was his religion. God had given these men the gift of free will, to make decisions to do something good and noble or to do something cruel, cowardly and vicious. Inspired by the devil, they made a decision to kill a Catholic young man – Ciaran Heffron – and duly carried out that killing.' Father O'Sullivan said the 'guilt would remain with the killers' and that Ciaran's blood lying on the ground outside the bus depot would 'cry to the Lord for justice'. Everyone I spoke to afterwards, including Ciaran's family, reported that Father O'Sullivan had done a marvellous job.

It was in the weeks and months after the funeral that I got to know Hugh and Teresa well. Of course, I had seen them coming to Mass regularly week after week and had said hello after the service, but until now I hadn't had the occasion to visit them.

The younger members of the family, Ciaran's brother Liam and sisters Sheila, Pauline and Angela, were extremely angry about Ciaran's murder. To their enormous credit, they weren't interested in revenge or retaliation, but, understandably, they wanted justice for Ciaran. They wanted his killers to be identified and apprehended and made to pay for their crime. His parents no doubt wanted the same thing, as did we all, but they weren't angry. Their son was dead, but they felt nothing. They were numb and their numbness troubled them, as if something were the matter with them, as if somehow they were at fault.

A short time after the funeral, maybe a few weeks later, I received a call from an official at the Northern Ireland Office. He explained that Secretary of State Mo Mowlam was keen to pay a private visit to the Heffron family to offer her condolences and pay her respects to them in person, but she didn't want to intrude on their grief. I was requested to approach the family and enquire if they would welcome such a visit. Hugh and Teresa said they would indeed welcome the visit, on the condition that I would agree to be present to help oil the cogs of social interaction.

As it turned out, my presence was hardly necessary, for Mo Mowlam was such a genuine, warm-hearted, down-to-earth person and she immediately put all of us at our ease. She wasn't in the least posh or stuffy. She knew that Teresa was suffering from cancer and as a fellow sufferer she was able to make an instant connection with her. Sitting there with her straggly thin hair growing back after cancer treatment, she confessed to us in good humour that she sometimes coped with the stress of being Secretary of State for Northern Ireland by having one or two whiskeys too many, and that at times her language could be colourful.

Before she left, I gave her a hug. She was a little taken

Teresa Heffron.

aback as, she explained, she wasn't used to being hugged by a Catholic, never mind a Catholic priest. It was a spontaneous gesture on my part. I hugged her because I felt thankful for all the positive benefits I felt she was bringing to our society, grateful for the gift of compassion she had brought to this hurting, grieving family, but most of all because she was a woman who was battling bravely with her own health issues and I felt moved to offer her that simple expression of human solidarity.

Not much more than a year after Ciaran's death and Mo's visit, Teresa died. As I reflect on Teresa's life and on my experience of her, I am struck by the extent to which she exemplified the qualities and values that Jesus spoke about in the Beatitudes, found in St Matthew's Gospel (5:3–10).

Jesus says, 'Blessed are the poor in spirit, for theirs is the kingdom of heaven.' Teresa was eminently poor in spirit. The loss of her health, the cruel loss of her son, Ciaran, and her motherly concern for the rest of her family made Teresa acutely aware of her need for God and her complete dependence on Him.

Every day Teresa talked to God about her concerns. Every day she visited the church to light a candle at Our Lady's shrine and say a prayer. Her faith in God's love was strong and, if anything, it became stronger as a result of the trials she experienced in her life. It was her faith that made her want so much to go to Lourdes with the diocesan pilgrimage in the month before she died, in order to pray for healing. It was that same faith which helped her to accept from God's hands the particular form of healing He chose to give her. In death, her healing at God's hands is complete.

Christ says, 'Blessed are those who mourn.' The last fifteen months of Teresa's life were very much a time of mourning. Teresa never got over Ciaran's death. It was something she lived with every day. She struggled not just with cancer but with a broken heart. The tears she shed were mostly silent ones. She bore her grief silently but still managed a smile for anyone she met. Even while bearing her own grief, Teresa's overriding concern was to give comfort and reassurance to her other children. God gave her precious time to do that. Now it is she who is being comforted.

Christ says, 'Blessed are the peacemakers'. Never once in all my visits to Hugh and Teresa did I hear either of them utter a word in bitterness or anger about Ciaran's death. Not long after Ciaran died, Teresa and Hugh took part in a cross-community outing to the Ulster Museum. They also attended the inter-church prayer service arranged that year as part of Crumlin Civic Week. In spite of their pain and confusion, they were determined that their suffering should not be used as an excuse for any behaviour that would damage community relations in the village. Their complete lack of bitterness and their commitment to peace in the community, in spite of what they suffered, was a shining example to the rest of us in the community at that time.

Christ says 'Blessed are the meek'. Teresa was a very meek and gentle person – so unassuming and softly spoken. These were lovely qualities that made her such a loveable person. For me it is this, her gentleness, that I remember most of all.

The lessons of Christ in the Beatitudes are written in Matthew's Gospel for anyone to read and learn. I was privileged to see them writ large also in the 'book' of the life of Teresa, and was moved by them.

Brigid and Dan's Story

When I came to Crumlin in 1997, the welcome I received from so many people meant a great deal to me. As I stood at the church door and greeted the parishioners after Mass, or as I walked up the main street in the morning on my way to buy a newspaper, people would stop and say, 'You're welcome to the parish, Father. I hope you will be happy here.' And I was.

No welcome could have been more sincere and warm than the one given to me by Brigid and Dan Trowlen. When I would visit their home each month to bring communion to Brigid's brother, 'Wee' Paddy Cardwell, Brigid would be sitting in her usual seat in the corner, ready for a chat and a bit of craic. Once in a while, if I wasn't under too much pressure, I would stay around for a cup of tea and a slice of Brigid's glorious homemade soda bread. And more than once, at Brigid's insistence, when I left their home it was with more of her soda bread tucked under my arm for later.

Once or twice I got into a conversation with Brigid where it soon became evident that she thought one thing and I thought another. She could be passionate about things. She was a feisty, spirited woman who knew her own mind and had no qualms about expressing it.

In the end she would often appear to come round to my way of thinking, but I suspect it was more out of an old-fashioned sense of deference to the collar than because I had managed to change her opinion. That's one of the things I liked so much about Brigid. You knew what she was thinking or feeling because she wore her heart on her sleeve. She was always open and honest about what she thought and believed. And being like that encouraged others in her company to be the same. With Brigid I felt I could let my hair down, so to speak. I felt I could be myself.

When Brigid passed away in August 1998, her husband Dan was heart-broken and he struggled bravely to come to terms with his grief. And then, less than two years later, Dan

Dan Trowlen.

himself was called to God. I was very fond of Dan. There was a lovely warmth to his personality. He had a kind, gentle way of speaking, and the light in his eye conveyed a capacity for good humour that was very endearing.

After Dan died, a letter came to light that he had written some nine months earlier. It was addressed to his family and was to be read by them in the event of his death. It began, 'There comes a time when one has to say goodbye for the last time, and this is the last time. There are just a few things I would like you to know when that time comes.'

What was it that caused Dan to write that letter nine months before he died? Maybe he was thinking about his dear wife Brigid, who had died the previous year. Or maybe it was the couple of angina attacks he'd had recently that made him think about his own death. In any case, at the time of writing that letter, death was on his mind, and he was thinking about his family and what he wanted to say to them.

The first part of the letter concerned practical arrangements for his funeral. It was the last part, however, that I found most interesting. Addressing his family, he said, 'Please live peacefully with one another, so that nothing that has passed, nothing here and now, and nothing that has to come, will come between you. As you were knit together in your mother's womb, please live peacefully as we were at 6 Lisburn Road, Glenavy.' And he finished off the letter with a touch of that gentle humour so familiar to all who knew him: 'Signed, your Da. Dress me in my best – might look better.'

When I read that letter for the first time, what struck me was that what Dan wanted for his family was so very similar to what Our Lord himself prayed for shortly before his death. Saint John records Jesus praying for his disciples, 'May they all be one, Father, as you and I are one.' On another occasion he said directly to his disciples, 'Peace be with you, my own peace I leave you.'

Unity and peace. These things that Our Lord wanted for his disciples are the very same things that Dan wanted for his family. Isn't that what we would all want for our families, for them to be united and at peace with one another? Clearly Dan's letter has a relevance that goes far beyond his own immediate family. It applies to all of us, emphasizing the need to pay attention to our family relationships and not to take them for granted.

We're all familiar with the saying that 'blood is thicker than water'. By that we acknowledge the unique bond which unites those who share the same flesh and blood. 'Flesh and blood' speaks to us of the unique relationship between parents and their children – it speaks of loyalty, commitment to nurture our children, to care for them and protect them, to stand by them, no matter what. That's how Dan was to his children and grandchildren – instinctively understanding, gentle, warm-hearted and wise.

But there is another, much deeper meaning to 'flesh and blood' than that. There is also the flesh and blood of Christ in the Eucharist. All those who share in the one flesh and blood of Christ, do they not also have a unique spiritual bond, a bond created by the Holy Spirit, that makes them brothers and sisters of Christ and of each other? Do they not, by virtue of that spiritual bond, have an obligation to care for and support one another as they would members of their own natural family?

Dan Trowlen was acutely aware of belonging to that wider faith family and of his obligations to it. I saw the practical consequences of that relationship many times. During the years I spent in Crumlin, I attended quite a number of wakes and funerals. Everywhere I went, Dan was there before me. I doubt there was a wake or a funeral in the parish that Dan didn't attend. He was a friend to everyone and he always did the right thing, particularly when people were bereaved. As for myself, visiting some houses for the first time and not knowing anyone, I was always glad to have Dan there to sit with and talk to.

Dan was someone who lived life to the full. I can still picture him on the dance floor of Saint Clare's, the parish hall, leaping around like a young lad until his body told him he wasn't one any more. For many years he was an enthusiastic and loyal member of Saint Joseph's Gaelic Club in Glenavy. He had a love for Gaelic football that took him all over Ireland in support of the Antrim county team. In fact, just a week before he died he was at the Antrim–Derry match, jumping up and down like the young fella he thought he was and shouting himself hoarse. Being deceased, of course, doesn't mean that you necessarily lose interest all of a sudden in the fortunes of your county team. I'm sure there is strong Trowlen support from the heavenly sidelines during county matches and, who knows, maybe even a bit of roaring and shouting as well – only in a holy way, of course.

Dan had a little prayer book that he used every day. It was so well-thumbed that in places the print had worn away and it was no longer possible to make out the words. There was one particular prayer he used to say every day. I remember he once pointed it out to me and told me how it gave him great strength. It's called 'the three o'clock prayer' and a little explanation is given beforehand that says this: 'Three o'clock, the hour of Our Lord's death, was a time of grace for the whole world – the moment when mercy triumphed over justice. Beg Jesus at this hour to have mercy on the poor souls who are about to die. No greater act of mercy can you pray for.'

The prayer itself goes like this:

You expired, Jesus, but the source of life gushed forth for souls and an ocean of mercy opened up for the whole world. O Fount of Life, unfathomable Divine Mercy, envelope the whole world and empty yourself out upon us. O Blood and Water, which gushed forth from the heart of Jesus as a fount of mercy on us, I trust in You.

That prayer, which Dan said every day, I offer now for him and for Brigid, for Harry McCluskey, for Ciaran Heffron and his mother Teresa, for Mo Mowlam, and for all those I have had the privilege to serve as their priest and who have completed their earthly pilgrimage. I could have written about any number of wonderful individuals, both living and dead, whose lives have taught me inspirational lessons. I am regularly humbled as I witness the amazing and manifold ways that goodness expresses itself in the lives of so many of those I meet.

I am deeply grateful for having known them; grateful, too, for the example of their lives and for the valuable lessons they taught me: the need for respect, reverence and humility in the face of creation and the world of nature; the need for courage, fortitude and perseverance in the face of life's difficulties and trials; that there can be dignity and grace in suffering; the importance of family and community, and the need to promote harmony and peace in our relations with others; the power of faith to support us in all the ups and downs of life; the joy of living this life to the fullest in whatever circumstances we find ourselves.

I realize that I have been richly blessed with some wonderful teachers in the university of life, among them Harry, Teresa, Brigid and Dan. Such as these are the salt of the earth. They made their mark and they made a difference to me. *Requiescant in pace*. May they rest in peace.

4

The Circle of Life

*A journey of a thousand miles must begin
with a single step.*

Lao Tzu, *Taoist philosopher*

Father David

EVERY ONCE IN A WHILE I develop an enthusiasm for a particular piece of music and it stays with me for days, or sometimes weeks. The music will play over and over in my head and I will hum or sing it in the shower, as you do, or while out walking or driving the car, or while simply pottering about the house. In the throes of my enthusiasm I might play the piece repeatedly, listening to it again and again, as, for example, I did in my youth when for a time I couldn't get enough of Fauré's Requiem, or in my teens when I discovered the Irish singer Mary Black, or Bernadette McGreevy singing Bach.

In the early nineties, the singer Michael Ball had a huge hit in the UK with the single 'Love Changes Everything' from Andrew Lloyd Webber's 1989 musical *Aspects of Love*. I heard it on the radio and developed an enthusiasm for it, so I wasted no time in purchasing the sheet music, and for the next few weeks I played and sang it over and over again at the old secondhand piano I had bought off a dealer in Gypsy Street.

At that time, I was a young priest, not long ordained, and teaching in Our Lady and St Patrick's College, a diocesan grammar school under the principalship of Father Paddy McKenna, with whom for seven years I happily shared a house at Kings Road in the Knock area of East Belfast. Each school day during lunch break I'd leave the school and drive the short distance to Kings Road for my lunch, which was prepared by Agnes, our Scottish housekeeper. Agnes's culinary strength, her pièce de résistance, was vegetable soup, and it was on account of this soup that Agnes had been poached from her previous employment in the college canteen by the former college principal, Father Joe Conway, who by all accounts was particularly partial to vegetable soup.

As well as sharing my love of singing, Agnes also shared the enthusiasm I had at that time for Lloyd Webber's 'Love Changes Everything'. Whenever I sat down at the piano, Agnes would abandon whatever she was doing in the kitchen and join me at the piano and together we would sing the song at the tops of our voices, Agnes unwittingly lending a comical flavour to the song with her strong Scottish accent. All we needed was an accordion accompaniment and the transformation from West End musical to Saturday night sing-along with wee Andy Lloyd McWebber down in the club would have been complete.

One lunch break, while Agnes and I were engaged in this activity, we were surprised by Father Paddy, who had arrived home early for his lunch – much to our embarrassment and to his obvious amusement.

Love changes everything. Three little words, and yet how true they are! For me, that statement expresses something of the essence of the message of Jesus of Nazareth. It's what he wanted us to know. No matter what difficulties, troubles and challenges a person might experience in life, if they have learned to love, and if they are fortunate enough to know the love of others and the love of God, it is possible to overcome the greatest tribulations that life and death may bring. And more than that: when people love one another, their love can change their world.

Enjoying tea and friendship at Hannahstown.

Time and time again, I have found this to be true in my own life. The love of family and of good friends, and above all the overwhelming love of God, has taught me an invaluable lesson. Love given and love received is the key to living a blessed and rich life, even in the midst of life's vicissitudes. To paraphrase another song, the greatest lesson you'll ever learn is simply to love and to be loved in return.

It is sometimes said that one of the greatest causes of stress is moving home. When a priest is moved by his bishop from one parish to another, he is not only moving house, he is also leaving behind a community where he has built up a network of supportive relationships and moving to an unfamiliar place where he is a stranger. When I came to Hannahstown parish in 2006, I found the transition very difficult. I had been very happy and contented in Whitehouse, my previous parish, and the bishop's decision to move me to a different parish had come as a great shock. In Hannahstown I knew no one and experienced considerable difficulties settling in. Six months into my new appointment, I still felt isolated and very much alone. There were times when I felt like calling in a removal company and getting them to pack up my stuff and take me anywhere, and dealing with the bishop and the consequences afterwards. Truth be told, I was feeling utterly miserable, and in spite of my best efforts to put on a happy face, I suppose my misery showed.

The first glimmer of light came one morning after a weekday Mass. Rose, one of the daily Mass-goers, stayed behind to speak to me. 'Father,' she said, 'I hope you don't mind me saying this, and I hope you won't misunderstand, but I just want you to know that I love you.' Now, it's not every day that a woman comes up to me and tells me that she loves me, and even though Rose is a wee grey-haired woman in her seventies (she won't mind me saying that) and therefore a profession of romantic love was unlikely to be on the agenda, I admit that I was initially somewhat taken aback. Seeing my confusion, Rose quickly went on to explain that she could see how unhappy I was and she wanted me to know that 'in God's name' she loved me. I should consider her a friend, and if there was ever anything she could do to help me, I only had to ask.

I don't know how long it took Rose to pluck up the courage to say those words. I wonder if she spoke on the spur of the moment, or if she had debated with herself for some time whether she should say them or not. Either way, her words to me that morning made all the difference, and it is a kindness I shall never forget. Love can be expressed in so many different ways and sometimes it changes everything, as it did for me that day. Rose was my first friend in Hannahstown and because of her I have been blessed with many more friends, whose encouragement and support has meant a great deal to me. Just as her act of kindness made all the difference to me at that time, so over the years love has made all the difference in her life. Rose shared with me something of her own story, and with her permission I shall share a little of that story now with you.

Rose's Story

Rose was born in Scotland. Her mother, who was eighteen when she married, died just three years later, when giving birth to Rose's younger brother, Jim. Rose's family life fell apart at that moment. Aged just fifteen months, Rose was brought to live with her paternal grandmother in Hannahstown in County Antrim, while Jim was taken to live with an aunt. For some years after that, her father drifted from Scotland through England in search of work and Rose saw and heard little of him. Once a year he would come home to visit for a weekend, but he would spend his time mostly in the pub. From a young age, Rose understood that her father never sent money to support them, and consequently money at home was scarce. Of love, however, there was no lack. Her grandmother was a very wise and loving woman.

One morning, when Rose was eleven years old, a letter arrived unexpectedly from her father. Enclosed was a photograph of him with his new bride. Rose felt angry and resentful that her father was choosing to make a new home and a new life elsewhere without her, but also confused that her grandmother seemed pleased about it. But as her grandmother explained, 'Now that he has a new wife and home we will know where to find him.'

When Rose was eighteen, she met and fell in love with Eddie, who three years later would become her husband. Like any young bride, Rose's head was filled with plans for a happy marriage and a family. She wanted four children and a nice home. When she fell pregnant, it looked as if God was smiling on them. But their dreams were short-lived. Rose lost the baby after just twelve weeks as a result of miscarriage. Naturally, Rose was deeply disappointed, but she was somewhat consoled when it was explained to her that many couples fail to carry their first child to full term and that miscarriage is not unusual. Putting their trust in God, she and Eddie tried again and were thrilled when Rose became pregnant with their second child. But their expectations and hopes were dashed yet again when Rose lost this baby too after only four months.

This was to become a recurring pattern as Rose and Eddie continued to try for a child of their own. At the news of every pregnancy their hopes were raised, only to be cruelly dashed. In all, Rose and Eddie lost twelve children, seven of them by miscarriage and five who were stillborn. On one occasion, Rose lay in hospital for three months to allow her the best chance of carrying her child to full term. A week before Christmas, she came home and was resting and taking things easy. On Christmas morning, she went into labour. She was brought into hospital and delivered a stillborn child. The doctor said to her, 'Rose, don't be crying, you'll be all right. Anyway, the baby would have been badly handicapped.' And Rose replied, 'I would have loved that child, handicapped or not.'

The deaths of all her children inevitably took their toll on Rose's health, on her faith and on her relationship with Eddie. There were many times when Rose was deeply depressed by the loss of her children and began to question God's care for them and His ways of doing things. But Eddie would always tell her, 'Don't worry, Rose, God knows what He is doing.' Eddie had a very strong faith in God and his faith was a great support and consolation to Rose during those dark days.

After losing their tenth child, Rose and Eddie decided that they would adopt a child. Once they had completed all the necessary checks and procedures it was with indescribable joy that they took home a little baby boy called Eamonn. As Rose said, Eamonn was 'the best thing that ever happened' to her, after Eddie.

At the beginning of the 1970s, the sectarian upheaval erupted that was to afflict Northern Ireland for the next thirty years. Many people were killed. Civic life was severely disrupted. Communities were torn apart. Whole communities were displaced as, in an effort at 'ethnic cleansing', those of 'the other faith' were driven out of their homes and forced to move into single-faith-identity ghettos. Almost everyone suffered in the Troubles in one way or another, whether they realized it at the time or not.

Like so many others, Eddie and Rose, who were living in Derriaghy at that time, were forced out of their home. After much searching, they came across a derelict house on the Glenside Road, in the outskirts of West Belfast. The house was situated on an elevated site which afforded beautiful wide-ranging views across the city of Belfast and much of County Down. On a clear day you could see all the way to the Mourne mountains, where the slopes of Slieve Donard sweep down to the sea. It was so beautiful and peaceful, and such a contrast to the home they had just left behind. At that time Eddie was working and doing well in his work as a haulage contractor and so they were able to pay cash for the house, but after making the initial purchase they had to scrimp and save to get electricity and water and a new roof so that they could live there comfortably. It took them years to make the home they always wanted.

In 1976, Eddie was struck down with an illness that the doctors were initially unable to identify. Frequent stays in hospital meant that he was no longer able to work. His haulage lorries were sitting idle and with no money coming in, Eddie and Rose had no choice but to sell them. As Eddie's health deteriorated so too did their financial circumstances and they came to depend on State benefits. In 1978, Eddie had his first operation and the surgeons discovered cancer in his bowel. He spent five months in hospital and had seven operations in all. At one point during that time, Eddie's health deteriorated to such an extent that he was given only ten more days to live. It was explained to Rose there was little more the doctors could do for him except to try one last drug. This would be Eddie's only chance. Without the treatment he would certainly die. But the drug carried risks and Rose would have to give her permission for the doctors to try it. With little choice, Rose gave her consent.

By the time Eddie returned home he weighed just seven stone. Although the drug had saved his life, it had caused some brain damage and as a result he was unable to walk unaided. He could only manage to take a few steps in the house with the aid of crutches and as his health declined further he became confined to a wheelchair. He was only thirty-nine years old.

What followed was a living nightmare that was to last for years. Eddie could not be left alone in the house in case he had a fall and so Rose was forced to give up work in order to care for him. It was a most difficult period for Rose as Eddie fell into a deep depression and wouldn't accept help. For a while he was very angry with God and the world. This was perhaps the most difficult aspect of Eddie's illness as he struggled so hard to understand why this was happening to him. Sometimes he took his anger and frustration out on Rose and young Eamonn. Rose tried hard to shield Eamonn from his father's annoyance, and for the sake of the boy, she struggled to put on a brave face. To the outside world she pretended that everything was fine and that they were coping well, but, as she now recalls, the reality was quite different. 'I don't know where God was in those days, but I do know that without Him I wouldn't be here today.'

For the next twenty-seven years, Rose continued to care for Eddie in their home. Throughout all the years of Eddie's illness, there were countless hospital visits and after a heart attack, Eddie had a triple bypass. He had to have nerve blocks done on his spine and was also given a pacemaker, which needed to be replaced three times.

Eddie died in 2003. He was in a coma and on a life-support system for the last twenty-nine days. Rose and Eamonn, who by now was married to Lisa, sat with him in the hospital day after day and watched him slowly dying. Over the course of that last month, his vital organs gradually closed down one by one. Of this most difficult time Rose says, 'I pray he didn't suffer and that he knew we were with him and loved him so much.' The family received enormous support from friends. Rose says, 'I didn't realize I had so many friends and I thank God for them all.'

Of that first year after Eddie died, Rose remembers little. It all went by in a kind of blur. She knows she went to the cemetery every day to visit Eddie's grave, to talk to him and ask him to guide her and tell her what to do. They had lived their lives together for forty-two years and during that time had shared so many ups and downs, but now she had to learn to live her life all by herself. She felt scared, afraid to make decisions by herself and lacking in confidence. Prayer became her main source of support and each day she asked God to guide her. She worried a lot about things and wished she could trust in God more and let Him take over.

One month after Eddie died, news came to her that her father, of whom she had seen so little over the years, was seriously ill in Manchester. It took a lot of courage for her to go and visit him, but somehow she managed to do it. She made the trip five more times before he died, and during the course of those visits, Rose came to a better understanding of her father and of the terrible choices he'd had to make for the good of his children. After the tragic death of his wife, he hadn't wanted to give his children up, but as a young man of twenty-four he'd had no means of caring for his newborn son and young daughter of fifteen months. He thought that by sending them to live with his mother and sister at Hannahstown he would be giving them the best opportunity in life. And as she finally came to know the love of her father, so in the end Rose came to love her father in return, and her seven half-brothers and sisters, too.

At Mass one weekend, Rose saw an advert in the parish bulletin for 'Beginning Experience', an organization that offers support and help to people who find themselves alone after a death, divorce or separation and who are struggling to adapt to their new circumstances. Rose began to go along to their meetings, where she told the others in the group how she felt so sad, lost and empty without Eddie and didn't know how to change that. Even though she had many good friends and they were so good to her, she still felt terribly lonely without Eddie. Her life was in a rut and she didn't know how to get herself out of it other than by doing what she was already doing and that didn't seem to be making a difference. She felt helpless, weighed down by the constant presence of an oppressive sadness that she couldn't manage to shake off. It was as if she was slowly dying a little bit more each day.

As Rose shared her story and listened to others telling theirs, she realized that in spite of their different circumstances, they were all in much the same boat. They experienced many of the same difficulties and struggles, felt the same feelings and were all working towards the same end. Rose drew strength and encouragement from her experience of sharing in a small group. As the weeks went by she gradually began to find a way out of her grief and move towards a new life.

Reflecting on her relationship with God over the years, throughout all the difficulties she had experienced – the loss of her children and the protracted illness and death of her beloved husband – Rose felt that she had maintained a very close relationship with God. If it hadn't been for that special closeness with God, she didn't know how she could have survived at all. During Eddie's illness they had begged God to help them get through it and He had answered their prayer, though perhaps not always in the way that they wanted or understood.

As she grew mentally and emotionally stronger, Rose began to reflect again on the loss of her twelve babies and the pain that this continued to cause her. In those days, after a miscarriage or a stillbirth, the remains of the baby were disposed of by the hospital. Consequently there was no grave where Rose could go to visit and remember her dead children. In addition to the great sadness she still felt over the loss of her babies, she also felt guilty that she had somehow neglected them by not having a headstone or monument of some kind erected in their memory.

At that time, it so happened that my attention had recently been drawn to the existence on the fringes of our parish cemetery of an unofficial burial ground for babies who had died before baptism and who had been denied the dignity of a Christian burial. The death of a child must surely be the most devastating experience that any parent can have and for their child to be denied a Christian burial, as sadly was often the case in bygone days, can only have compounded the sorrow and anguish of those parents. Aware of this, and in the light of Rose's story and the stories of other women and parents like her, I felt the time had finally come for the issue to be decisively addressed.

The first step was to have a ceremony of consecration in order that those areas formerly outside the boundaries of the cemetery, which contained the remains of those babies who had died before baptism, would now be included. This was done at the annual Cemetery Sunday Mass for the blessing of graves in May 2008, which was attended by several thousand mourners. The second step was to arrange for a suitable monument to be erected within the cemetery area, a memorial to all babies and children who had died in whatever circumstances, whether before or after birth. It would be a quiet, private place where parents could come and sit a while to remember and pray.

A statue representing a father, mother and child was commissioned and paid for by public subscription. A considerable contribution towards the cost of the statue was received from the friends and family of Gerard Kane, a young man from the parish who had been tragically killed in a road accident at the age of twenty-one. The monument was finally erected and dedicated after Mass on the feast of All Souls, 2008, at which Rose and many other parents were present. Despite the simplicity of its design, the statue manages to convey all the love and tenderness of a mother towards her child as well as the strong, protective presence of a loving father.

During the service, we recalled the teaching of Jesus from St Mark's Gospel, 10:13–16:

People were bringing little children to him in order that he might touch them; and the disciples spoke sternly to them.

But when Jesus saw this, he was indignant and said to them, 'Let the little children come to me; do not stop them; for it is to such as these that the kingdom of God belongs. Truly I tell you, whoever does not receive the kingdom of God as a little child will never enter it.' And he took them up in his arms, laid his hands on them, and blessed them.

And we prayed:

Lord Jesus, tender Shepherd of the flock, our little ones now lie cradled in your love. Soothe the hearts of all parents who mourn for the loss of their child and bring peace and healing to their lives. Make their faith strong and give hope to their hearts.

Loving God, grant mercy to your family in their times of suffering. Comfort them with the knowledge that their little ones live with you and with your Son, Jesus Christ and the Holy Spirit, for ever and ever. Amen.

As Rose recalls it, the ceremony brought to the surface strong feelings of sadness and loss, but it was also an occasion of deep healing. Rose continues to visit the baby memorial regularly and remembers her little ones who are with God.

Rose's story has a happy ending. Her son Eamonn and daughter-in-law Lisa had a little girl called Nicole, who brings her great joy and happiness.

Nearly five years after Eddie's death, Rose wrote him this letter:

My dear Eddie,

How I love you. I hope you always knew this. I always used to say to you, 'I love you,' and I wanted you to say the same thing to me. Many, many times you did say it, but sometimes you used to say to me, 'I love you two and six.' I didn't understand what you meant and you explained, 'You love me, Rose, but I am telling you that I love you two and six – twice as much and six times more.' That was your way, Eddie.

I lived our forty-two years of marriage to the best of my ability. Yes, we had many rocky moments, but you and I made a promise to each other on our wedding day never to go to sleep on an argument. I think we always kept that promise. One or other of us always made the first move by putting an arm around the other. That's all it took, Eddie, for me to know that we were all right.

In the early days of our marriage, we went out on Saturday nights a lot. You were always the life and soul of the party. I must say to you that many a time I was jealous when you talked and sang to all the girls. Sometimes I would try to get someone interested in me because you always had a crowd around you. Thank God those feelings only lasted a short time.

We were so lucky that we always stuck together. In those days when I wanted a baby so much and it always ended in miscarriage, I was devastated and I used to think that you didn't care. When I wondered aloud about all this loss of life, you used to say to me, 'Rose, look at all the fun we are having trying.' I didn't always think this was funny though I realize you were only trying to cheer me up. When I was told by my doctor to have a little break from trying for a child, you didn't always want to do that. One time when I made arrangements to go to marriage guidance you went mad and I had to go by myself. I don't think, Eddie, that you would agree with me going to the Beginning Experience meetings and with the sharing and so on. You were always such a private person and believed that we could work out our own problems.

But Eddie, I am not as strong a person as you were. I really enjoy the Beginning Experience and have made so many friends. On the closing day I am going to say, 'Eddie, I am going to do my best to live my new life. Please don't forget to pray for me that I may be kept on the straight path.' How I miss you, your friendship, your wit and your company. But it is nearly five years since you died and with help I have survived. I am proud to say I was your wife.

I used to think that we were so lucky that you took sick while we were still together, as part of me wondered whether, if our life had gone on in the fast lane, we would have succeeded. I like to think we would. I hope you were as happy as I was. This is my letter of 'goodbye' to our marriage, Eddie. I ask you always to guide me from heaven to do what is right. Thank you, Eddie, for all our ups and downs. Yes, we had some hard times, but, thank God, we always muddled through.

Eddie, I must tell you, love, that you would have been very proud of Eamonn and Lisa. The whole month, the last month of your life, while you were lost in a coma, they were there for both of us. And when you died, I would have been completely lost without Eamonn. He turned out to be the son that you always wanted. You would be so proud of him. He still helps me out at Glenside as much as he can, even though he now has his own wife and home and garden to take care of, and also, surprise, surprise ... little Nicole, thank God. I wish you had been spared to know her. She is truly a gift from heaven.

As I read back over Rose's story, I am full of gratitude for her remarkable generosity in sharing her personal story not only with me, but through me with you, the reader. Rose wanted me to tell her story in the hope that her experiences might give some comfort, consolation and hope to others. It is typical of her that she should think that way. It's often said that life is a great teacher. If that is so, then Rose has been a great student. She has learned its lessons well.

As I come to the end of this story, I recall the love I have experienced in my own life from family, friends and strangers, and how the experience of that love has changed everything. I am reminded of St Paul's beautiful and inspiring passage on the nature of Christian love. I often use this text during wedding ceremonies because it seems so suitable when a couple are committing themselves to love one another 'for better, for worse . . . until death'. But, of course, this is intended to be a teaching for us all. I propose it to you for your own quiet reflection.

Be ambitious for the higher gifts. And I am going to show you a way that is better than any of them.

If I have all the eloquence of men or of angels, but speak without love, I am simply a gong booming or a cymbal clashing. If I have the gift of prophecy, understanding all the mysteries there are, and knowing everything, and if I have faith in all its fullness, to move mountains, but without love, then I am nothing at all. If I give away all that I possess, piece by piece, and if I even let them take my body to burn it, but am without love, it will do me no good whatever.

Love is always patient and kind; it is never jealous; love is never boastful or conceited; it is never rude or selfish; it does not take offence, and is not resentful. Love takes no pleasure in other people's sins but delights in the truth; it is always ready to excuse, to trust, to hope, and to endure whatever comes.

Love does not come to an end.

1 Corinthians 12:31–13:8

Father Eugene

I have always had an interest in law. Indeed, before deciding to study for the priesthood I had thought of studying law and had applied to some universities to do just that. I also thought of pursuing a career in music and/or theatre. But nothing came of these plans, and I decided to give the priesthood first refusal – and here I am!

That said, in 1987, a year after my ordination, I was asked by my Bishop if I would be interested in returning to Rome to study Church (Canon) law. How happy an 'accident' was that? By coincidence or providence – call it what you will – I got the chance to study something I had always been interested in and to return to Rome, a city I loved. To be frank, it was never going to be a great burden.

The reason why I was asked to study Church law was because several local Dioceses needed additional qualified and trained personnel to work in the local Church Tribunal, which, like similar Church Tribunals around the world, deals with those situations where a marriage has broken down irretrievably and where one party has approached the Church looking for an annulment – that is, a formal declaration and recognition by the Church that the marriage has been proved to be invalid.

This might all sound somewhat technical, and to a degree it is, but a simple example might help to illustrate it. If a person marries another person not for love or to be married in the ordinary sense of the word, but for the sole purpose of getting a passport or permanent residence rights in a particular country, then that marriage cannot be said to be a marriage as understood by the ordinary man in the street, nor, indeed, by the Church, which understands marriage to be a lifelong commitment based on mutual love and respect and freely chosen by the spouses.

In the Church tradition to which I belong, a marriage is presumed to be valid until proved otherwise. So, in order to provide a place or forum where a person can present proofs which they believe will overturn the presumption of validity, the Church provides a Tribunal where a person may present his or her claim and proofs of invalidity, and where qualified and trained personnel can render an independent decision.

The three years of study of Canon law (in Latin) turned out to be the most difficult and demanding years I had experienced either as a seminarian or as a post-graduate priest. But those years of study, and the experience I have gained since then in the area of marriage preparation and in the Church Tribunal, have been truly rewarding in ways I never expected.

Over the past twenty years I have met hundreds of people whose marriages have broken down irretrievably. There is a sense of loss for all concerned, including the extended family circle, sometimes accompanied by bitterness and resentment, especially where one party or side of the family places the blame for the failure of the marriage on the estranged spouse. Apportioning blame or scapegoating rarely, if ever, helps in the aftermath of marital breakdown. It's neither fair nor wise to point the accusing finger, for as the saying goes, 'When you point the finger at another, remember that three other fingers of the same hand are pointing back at you.' Having said that, valid reasons often surface to explain why a particular relationship has broken down. Sometimes the reasons are obvious and sometimes they are not so obvious. Whatever the situation, the breakdown of a relationship is a painful matter. Whatever the statistics – and the statistics are high – marital breakdown always leaves its mark, both psychological and spiritual.

In the course of my work in the Tribunal, I have met many individuals whose marriages began with great enthusiasm and hope, but then, for complex reasons, collapsed amidst bitter disappointment and recrimination. At the other extreme, I've met people who found themselves forced into marriage because of an unplanned pregnancy, or who married under pressure of one kind or another. Then there are those who married when they were extremely immature, and others whose partners carried on extra-marital affairs – which is completely contrary to the nature of marriage, and plainly unjust and unfair to one's spouse.

People naturally find it difficult to talk about their personal situation when they or their partner have failed to come up to the mark and have fallen short of the ideal set by tradition, Church teaching or others' expectations. Unlike the divorce process, which is not really designed to understand or facilitate the telling of the deeper human story behind the breakdown of a marriage, people have told me that they have found the annulment process to be healing in many ways. It's not guaranteed, but the possibility for some degree of healing is there for those – and there are many – who find the encounter a therapeutic one, providing a forum where they can tell their story, often for the first time, and be heard, understood and assured of God's continued love for them as they face a painful transition in their lives.

In many ways, coping with a broken marriage can be as

traumatic as bereavement, and in some ways it can be even harder. It is one thing to say farewell to a partner at a funeral, but it is quite another to close the door on a relationship, especially if there are children, and to know that your former partner has 'moved on' without you. It must be a kind of living death. Thank goodness, nowadays, there are many groups and societies that can offer support and advice in these circumstances. Church and State have their complementary structures and systems.

For some it might be that initial conversation with a friend or a pastor that begins the process, but inner healing, regret for wrongs done and forgiveness for wrongs experienced doesn't just happen overnight. Inner spiritual and psychological healing, similar to the physical healing of a cut, a bruise or a broken bone, can take much longer than expected, and, invariably, much longer than we would like, but healing of the pain of marital breakdown has to begin somewhere. 'Remember, it is those who had endurance that we say are the blessed ones.' (Letter of James, 5:11)

Alone with none but thee, my God, I journey on my way.
What need I fear when thou art near, Oh King of night and
　　day.
More safe am I within thy hand,
Than if a host did round me stand.

St Columb of Derry

Some years ago, I attended a conference at a Catholic retreat in London, in relation to my pastoral work. It was an occasion for us to share experiences, compare and contrast circumstances and to learn from them. All very laudable and professional, as you might expect. It was January and the days were cold and wet. Before I travelled to London for the conference, whatever virus I had contracted over Christmas was incubating nicely in my system, waiting to surface at the end of the conference.

My original intention was to stay on in London for a few days to enjoy a couple of shows in the West End. Alas, my plans came to nothing. I came down with an unmerciful cold, which could be described more precisely as 'man flu', and simply had to take to my bed. For this to happen in one's own home would have been bad enough, but for it to happen in a strange environment, far away from family and friends, was a most unpleasant experience. In an institutional environment, such as the one I was in, I knew it would be possible to extend my stay, but I was in no fit state to go to the dining room to eat or to take care of more personal issues, like washing or medication. I was pretty miserable, if truth be told. I had been looking forward to a few extra days in London to enjoy the theatre and here I was, a complete stranger, laid up in a Catholic retreat, sick and conscious of being a burden to others. Boarding school, like the one I attended as a boy, undoubtedly gives you some survival skills, but when you're sick and unable to fend for yourself you certainly feel vulnerable and alone.

You can imagine my relief and gratitude when a virtual stranger took it upon himself to come to my rescue, and to this day I am not sure whether this man fully realized how much I appreciated his help when I was sick and alone. I also feel a little guilty that I didn't show greater appreciation at the time for what he did. Maybe if he reads this book he'll recognize himself and realize how grateful I feel. I do hope so, because this is my opportunity to say thank you for being there when I needed help. That help, over those five long days, extended to making sure I had food when I was hungry and able to eat, plenty of water to drink, a companion to talk to, appropriate medication, a bath, and a few prayers when I was unable to say them myself. The care offered to me when I was sick and far from home has made me appreciate all the more the kindness and consideration that can so often be taken for granted, but which can make a world of difference to those in need.

In my work as a priest, just like many other priests the world over, I visit the sick and housebound of my small parish on a regular basis. In many ways I am very fortunate. While I work in the local Church Tribunal each day during normal office hours, I have an extension to my ministry as a priest in the parish. In addition to being available for Mass and the administrative responsibilities that are part and parcel of parish life, I visit the sick and housebound of the parish on the first Friday of every month, in accordance with the practice and tradition of Catholic devotion to the Sacred Heart of Jesus.

The number of people on my sick list are perhaps fewer than those in a bigger parish, but they are no less important for that. In some ways I am the envy of many fellow priests, as my small list of housebound parishioners allows me the opportunity to spend that little bit of extra time with them, which my colleagues with their greater numbers of the housebound simply cannot manage. That is a blessing both for me and for the people I visit, and it makes my visits to them in their homes or when they have to go to hospital all the more special.

We live in a society where the care and attention of nurses and doctors are, sadly, often taken for granted. A cleric's role is also frequently taken for granted. Speaking for the latter category, we are accustomed to that and to some degree expect it, but experience has taught me that we should never take the professionalism and care of doctors and nurses for granted.

My mother's long battle with heart failure in the last six to seven years of her life taught me to value the work of the medical professionals who looked after her and extended her life through innovative medical procedures. Without them, and, in particular, without the care and attention of one doctor, we would have lost our much-loved mother several years before her actual death.

Our mother knew that too, and that is why we, as a family, can never be thankful enough for the kindness, care and professionalism of the doctors, nurses and care assistants in our hospitals, care homes and auxiliary home-based services. We have a lot to learn from them, and from those who, out of kindness and generosity, teach us how wonderful it is to care for another human being and how thankful we should be in return.

I will praise you, Lord, you have rescued me
And have not let my enemies rejoice over me.

O Lord, I cried to you for help
And you, my God, have healed me.
O Lord, you have raised my soul from the dead,
Restored me to life from those who sink into the grave.

Sing psalm to the Lord, you who love him,
Give thanks to his holy name.
His anger lasts but a moment; his favour through life.
At night there are tears, but joy comes with the dawn.

Psalm 29

We live in a busy, sometimes frenetic world of activity. Many people are judged by their industry, efficiency and output. There is something inherently positive about setting goals and targets, but when these become ends in themselves they tend to be dehumanizing and turn us into machines. We are far from being machines. Love of music must be one of the great humanizing elements in life. Music has often been called an international language because it transcends all boundaries of race, religion, colour and culture. In my own life, it has been a daily source of joy and has played a significant part in helping me to make lasting friendships with people from walks of life very different from my own.

For many years, I have had the good fortune to be involved in opera and musical theatre, frequently, though unfairly, dismissed as 'am-dram'. But whatever it might be called by others, my experience of meeting and getting to know people through musical theatre has been fantastic.

Living in Northern Ireland through the height of the

Troubles from the seventies to the nineties has left its mark on many individuals and communities. However, despite the internal strife in Northern Ireland over the past thirty years, some experiences have been positive and uplifting. Making music together – both within and across our own communities – has been an enduring feature of life here; it brings people from very different backgrounds together and allows them to get to know one another in an environment where all are equal, all are valued and all are encouraged to mix without fear, apprehension or suspicion.

When describing the effects of my involvement in music-making with groups, societies and individuals, I have often called it 'practical ecumenism'. The emphasis here is on getting on with the job without getting bogged down in theory or speculation about the possible effects, both positive and negative, that such collaboration might have on people from different religious, political and cultural backgrounds. For me, if people can sing or play an instrument, then there's plenty of scope for them to get together and make music. OK, I know I'm fortunate that I can sing, but I feel *really* fortunate to have been able to pursue my love of music and to study singing techniques which have enabled me to become involved in all kinds of musical activities.

I'm also a Catholic priest, and in Northern Ireland that kind of identity tag might, in some circles, cancel out any inherent value I might bring to an encounter with others, simply because I represent something different, something alien or foreign to another person or community's outlook. This might sound bizarre, even medieval, to some, but it has been the reality on the ground where I have grown up and where I live. Thankfully, my experience has been quite the opposite, because

A parish wedding rehearsal turns into choir practice with Father Eugene.

music, not the Church, has been the point of contact. My being a priest has been secondary to being a musician, and that has not been a bad thing. Through music I have become aware of the joys and struggles of other people from a variety of backgrounds, all different from my own. Similarly, they have been introduced to my world and to my experiences as a working priest, in a world where faith and belief in God is often questioned, challenged, or even dismissed altogether.

Music has allowed all of us, whatever our backgrounds, to ask the questions we have always wanted to ask but have perhaps been afraid to. Through music I have made new friends and I know I am the richer for the experience. Sharing the love of music has led to sharing at a personal level, and that brings joy and a sense of appreciation – and of being appreciated – that is impossible to put into words. Maybe that's why God has given us the gift of music!

We all carry within us various experiences and images of loneliness, like picture postcards: ones we've seen on TV, in newspapers and advertisements, ones conjured up in our imagination, from our own experiences or from meeting people who tell us quite candidly that they feel lonely. Yet we might never wish to admit even to ourselves, let alone to others, that we have been lonely in the past or that we currently harbour feelings of loneliness and isolation. Somehow, loneliness suggests failure. To have many friends, to be in a fulfilling relationship and to be constantly in the company of others is seen as a mark of success, the opposite of loneliness, or so we're led to believe. Yet the simple truth is, one can be lonely in a marriage, in a city full of people, in the company of others, in youth, in old age, in poverty or in wealth; loneliness is no respecter of individuals and it can affect anyone, regardless of age or personal circumstances. Even the thought of being lonely scares us.

Despite having survived seven years at boarding school, where homesickness fed on childhood fears and anxieties, I have only ever felt truly lonely once in my adult life. Am I lucky? I think so, for I remember well the effect it had on my mood and how this awful sense of isolation affected how I related to others, even though they were completely unaware of what I was experiencing. That's the mystery and pain of loneliness – no one need ever know!

I am no psychologist, psychiatrist or trained counsellor, but as a human being with some experience of meeting people at vulnerable moments in their lives, I can only assume that we have all experienced or will experience loneliness at some time, which can best be described as a real sense of emptiness and negativity. But perhaps there's another way of looking at this 'problem' – a way of harnessing the beneficial effects of solitude, which is very different from loneliness, in order to have a more positive experience. For solitude can help us to create space and time for quiet reflection, thought, prayer and rest. The thing about modern life is that solitude is often presented as something to be afraid of, something to be avoided at all costs, something that should be reserved for the enclosed convent or the monastery. So we fall into the trap of filling our days with activity and thereby avoid even the merest chance that we might have to face being on our own for longer than we would like. We end up being driven and shaped by our constant activity, leaving no space in our lives for a quiet interlude, from which we could emerge refreshed.

Now, of course, I fully acknowledge that loneliness is not solitude, and that it can cause pain and alienation. Is there a cure? Or is this something we just have to learn to live with? Perhaps it is. I think of the many elderly people whose spouses, friends and contemporaries have died, leaving them behind to live with their memories but not able to share them with others. There are many whose ill health sets them apart from the mainstream of daily life or who have to battle daily with depression, which I think is the manifestation of loneliness at its worst. There's the spouse or partner who feels lonely and neglected in a relationship that promised to be life-giving, but which is now so different, so painful. There's the person in prison, whether justly or unjustly deprived of liberty, who knows what it is like to be shut out and separated from normal society. And then there's the example of Christ, who in his suffering felt abandoned by God his Father, but into whose hands he commended his spirit. But perhaps one way of alleviating loneliness is simply to reach out to others; we can offer a helping hand or just a few moments of our time to listen to those who may need a friend. A little compassion can go a very long way and can make a huge difference to those in need.

Prayer for Those Living Alone

I live alone, dear Lord, stay by my side,
In all my daily needs be Thou my guide.
Grant me good health, for that indeed I pray,
To carry on my work from day to day.
Keep pure my mind, my thoughts, my every deed,
Let me be kind, unselfish in my neighbour's need.
Spare me from fire, from flood, malicious tongues,
From thieves, from fear, and evil ones.
If sickness or an accident befall,
Then humbly, Lord, I pray hear Thou my call,
And when I'm feeling low, or in despair,
Lift up my heart and help me in my prayer.
I live alone, dear Lord, yet have no fear,
Because I feel Your Presence ever near.
Amen.

Anon

I Cannot Do This Alone

O God, early in the morning I cry to you.

Help me to pray

And to concentrate my thoughts on you:

I cannot do this alone.

In me there is darkness,

But with you there is light;

I am lonely, but you do not leave me;

I am feeble in heart, but with you there is help;

I am restless, but with you there is peace.

In me there is bitterness, but with you there is patience;

I do not understand your ways,

But you know the way for me.

Restore me to liberty,

And enable me to live now

That I may answer before you and before me.

Lord, whatever this day may bring,

Your name be praised.

Dietrich Bonhoeffer

Father Martin

There is an ebb and flow to life's journey, driven by our emotions and experience. From the very first moment of our existence, we begin to engage in a unique experience, which will cast its light and its shadow over us. Our relationship with the world, ourselves and God is finely balanced.

Certain aspects of my life have, I know, been very influential in terms of the person I have become and the path I have chosen to take. As a twin, for example, I am sure I have learned to share space more easily than some, but I am always conscious that my birth was somewhat traumatic; as I was being delivered into this world the cord tightened around my neck, and I owe my life to the care and expertise of the hospital staff who delivered me safely into the hands of my mother. I often wonder what it must have felt like as a newborn to gasp for breath, and whether that experience has in any way shaped my desire to value life in all its complexity, to savour every moment.

As I have mentioned before, growing up in a not very affluent family in Northern Ireland meant that we didn't have much in the way of material possessions, but we learned to appreciate the simple things that life could offer us. There was a sense of having time, of being able to savour things without rushing, of making sense of the world. I recall my childhood being one of space, imagination, camaraderie, dependence and reassurance, all underpinned by the wonderful certainty that we were loved and cherished.

The memories of seemingly insignificant moments serve to reinforce the gentle nature of my childhood: gathering blackberries along an overgrown lane, dipping my toes into a babbling stream, eating the freshly baked bread made by one of our neighbours, Mrs Kelly, the recollection of which seems ingrained in my taste buds!

But it's too easy to look back at life through rose-tinted glasses. In reality, the shadow lands were also there, even if only in the form of petty arguments or childish rivalries which inevitably ruffled feathers and made life difficult at times. But I know now that life's journey was never intended to be smooth and without its difficulties, and looking back I can see that the problems that seemed so big and important as a child – and which now seem so trivial – were building blocks that I needed to negotiate and overcome if I was to learn how to cope in adulthood. This, I believe, is true for all young people as they embark on the great adventure that is growing up. We all have to navigate our way through the rough and gentle seas of life.

School and Church both exerted considerable influence on me as a child, and faith was very much at the heart of both experiences. This early influence undoubtedly laid the foundations for my vocation later in life.

As far as the children were concerned, we were all of us wee rogues at times, although we also enjoyed more serious games, such as pretending to celebrate Mass and holding imitation processions. We would become quite excited when the local priest came to call; the 'good room' would be used for the special occasion and we'd all try to be on our best behaviour. But I also remember not paying too much attention to what was going on in church and playing with my father's cap during the Sunday service. I would sit next to him and all the men would be seated on the right, with the women on the left. I could never really understand the need for this division, and I'm glad that we no longer feel the need to keep to this tradition.

I enjoyed my school days and still remember the personalities there and the activities we did: the joy of lessons about art and nature, as well as my sore fingertips as I prodded the page – all too well deserved after my poor efforts in our spelling tests!

Life was simple where we lived in the countryside at Hillcrest, outside the village of Claudy, where the cow and sheep sales took place. I remember people coming to get water from our pump, a man coming to sharpen our knives, and the bread man, Gene Burke, who filled my mother's arms with bread and sometimes had a special treat for us children. Little did I know then how soon this world would change, overwhelmed by the looming dark clouds of what was initially in the late sixties the positive message of the Civil Rights Movement, but soon became a catastrophic sequence of events.

My first experience of the army was when, as children, we used to wave to passers-by at the bottom of our garden. On one occasion an army lorry drove past; the driver waved, then lost control and headed for the hedge. I remember us all scattering like birds on the road and diving for cover.

When we moved to Derry in the early seventies, the upheaval was devastating for me and I empathize with anyone who is anxious about taking new avenues in life, or who might resist change. I could not bear to leave behind my friends and neighbours, or the place that had been my world, my kingdom. It's ironic that, as a priest, this sense of 'letting go', of almost constant change, would become a pretty frequent experience throughout my adult life.

At the time, I had to face the unknown when I came to Derry, and I literally kicked and screamed my way into Primary 5. It was a painful time. The move was further complicated by the new city atmosphere and the smoke-filled air, which reflected all the bombing and the violent attacks –

even murder – that was part and parcel of the new landscape that I found myself in. It was a world away from the relative peace and tranquillity of Claudy, and the adjustment I had to make was painful and quite traumatic for me. Luckily, music proved to be a significant means of escape for me and the family; it was a release from the everyday reality that surrounded us – particularly the very harsh reality of fear and suspicion that followed Bloody Sunday.

Our parents tried to make sure that our lives were as normal as they could possibly be in the circumstances, but the constant bag and body searches, the questions and the unnerving presence of both police and army undoubtedly shaped our lives as security became a real issue. But throughout this traumatic time the Church continued to exert its influence and my sense of vocation continued to develop, despite – or perhaps because of – this difficult situation.

I remember walking home to our new house one day and being stopped by someone much bigger than myself, who asked 'Are you a taig?' – a derogatory term used for Catholics, but which meant nothing to me at the time. Luckily I got away scot free, although I was terrified by the encounter. This was my first experience of the gulf that can exist between people from different backgrounds and faiths. My parents always taught us all to respect everyone, whatever their background or their faith, and this wonderful lesson of tolerance has stayed with me throughout my life.

The move to Garron Tower at the age of eleven was also quite traumatic for me. Once I had settled into our new house, I was quite content to stay close to home, to play and help in the garden, and generally help to keep things neat and tidy. Now I felt I had to go through a major upheaval all over again, and quite frankly, I dreaded it. I really loathed change – and as you have probably gathered by now, it is something I still struggle with! But here I was again, propelled into an unfamiliar situation, even though my brother Eugene had made the leap ahead of me and would help me to make the transition.

I found the first year at Garron Tower well-nigh impossible to cope with, as I suffered from terrible homesickness. The college was (and still is) beautiful and the staff were very supportive, but I was growing and grappling with change in every sense. It was the first time I had experienced loneliness, though it was not to be the last. There were probably many other boys who felt just the same way I did, but emotions could not be easily expressed in that very male-dominated society. I was helped a great deal by Sister Marie Gertrude and Father McKavanagh, whose music lessons gave me confidence, as well as by others such as Mr Hughes, Mr Anderson and many more, whose humanity came shining through. The priests were loyal, dedicated and prayerful men who had sacrificed much and who were rewarded by the way the school grew in stature and drew so many people.

Throughout my time at college my faith grew, despite times of doubt. But I have come to understand that doubt can be a good thing, as it calls you to question and think about all manner of issues and problems until, ultimately, you are able to work through and refine what you truly believe in.

Looking back, these school years were extremely formative and influential for me, not least because of the doubts and questions they raised. Throughout this time, the call to the priesthood continued to grow – like a constant echo in my mind and heart – and the retreats I attended served to encourage and guide me further. I remember reaching a significant crossroads when, in my last year at school, I decided to try the priesthood. I still had lots of questions, and was not really sure what I was letting myself in for, but the decision was made, and for once I was able to look forward to a new adventure – albeit with a little trepidation!

A few years ago I went on a retreat with some colleagues, and I recall one of the exercises we were asked to take part in. It involved photos being placed on the ground and us being asked to choose one that stood out and 'spoke' to us. My mother had died not long before this, so I was feeling quite vulnerable at the time. I picked up a photo of a boy sitting on a train and waving goodbye through the window, and quite suddenly I was overwhelmed by a sense of intense sorrow. I went to bits. The sensation of letting go swept over me and the memory of saying goodbye rocked me as the tears began to flow. I was reliving what I had experienced from an early age, when each letting go, each parting, had felt like a bereavement.

Joan and Frank, Father Martin and Father Eugene's parents, at the family home in Derry.

Today, I always try to encourage people to express how they feel because this release can be enormously helpful in the healing process.

A whole new world opened up for me at university. I loved the variety of life, the intermingling of people from different backgrounds, the new friends I made and the way in which music could help to build bridges with so many. I embarked upon a disciplined existence in terms of study, and yet music was always there to lift my spirits and ease my days, thank God. I loved Queen's and the subjects I was studying, and felt as if my mind was being stretched to the limit as I grappled with the mysteries of life. Father McEvoy in the Scholastic Department opened up new horizons for me, and in Ancient History I learned about civilizations whose influence I could see when I had the opportunity to travel to Rome as a student. And then there were my music lessons with Frank Capper, a truly gifted man who had such a wonderful capacity to bring out the best in his students.

I have no doubt that God sends people into our lives to encourage us and help us to grow and develop. The musical journey I embarked on in my youth has been of profound importance to me throughout my life and has helped me to grow as an individual. I feel that there has been a sense of

Providence in all of this and recognize that learning how to interpret music has helped me to realize how important it is to interpret life in all its shades and colours.

Although I felt sad to leave Queen's University, a new chapter opened up for me at the Irish College in Rome. Discovering Rome was a joy: my eyes were like saucers when I first beheld the city in all its grandeur. The influence of the Catholic Church was evident everywhere and soon my colleagues and I were making friends with students of other nationalities in the other seminaries. There was a sense of common purpose, of us all journeying together towards a shared goal. In many ways my faith was deepened by the challenges I faced in Rome, as I struggled with a new language and developed new friendships, feeling vulnerable on the one hand and excited on the other.

On our days off I feasted my eyes on art and architecture, visiting the catacombs, art galleries, churches where saints are buried and honoured, and all things ancient. As I settled into a routine of studying, my own understanding also began to flourish, and I became curious to find out more and more. Of course, there were times of loneliness and solitary moments, but good friends were a source of comfort and support. I think we collectively came to understand that we were all in the same situation, and this certainly helped us to overcome our problems.

I recall how we all went travelling together at Christmas as we were not allowed to return home to our families. This sense of being dependent upon each other, and living so far from home and loved ones at such a special time of year, helped us to forge strong, supportive friendships which, I'm delighted to say, continue to this day.

While I was in Rome I was given the wonderful opportunity to sing at papal ceremonies in the Vatican, particularly at Christmas and Easter. It was during one of these ceremonies that some of my colleagues and I had the chance to meet Pope John Paul II. This was both a privilege and an honour. He always struck me as a humble and gracious man whose love of Christ and love of the Church shone through. He seemed to have his feet firmly on the ground and displayed a real warmth of character. I had seen him once before, in Galway when I was in my late teens; he had inspired me before I went into the seminary and continued to do so throughout my priestly life.

In 1988, I decided not to be ordained as a deacon at the same time as my colleagues. Indeed, two of us decided not to go forward at this time. I knew I simply was not ready. I needed stillness and time to reflect on the implications such an important decision would have on the rest of my life. After further reflection, I was ordained to the deaconate back home in Derry at the Good Shepherd Convent on 29 September 1988, on the feast of the Archangels. Ordination to the priesthood took place the following year, on 9 July 1989.

The priesthood has undoubtedly been challenging and I have found myself in many difficult situations over the last twenty-one years. I am now in my ninth parish of Newtownards and Comber.

During my time as a priest I have spent seventeen years in special ministry. This involved working in Marriage Tribunal and, more recently, Catechesis, which meant that I would travel around the schools of the Diocese, meeting staff and pupils and providing courses and advice on the programme for Religious Education. Throughout these years I was still living and working within my own busy parish – so much to do and there always seemed to be so little time!

Ministering as a priest means that you have to wear many hats as there are so many different scenarios to deal with. There is liturgy, prayer and spiritual matters, of course, as well as the business of finance, the maintenance and restoration of buildings, school affairs and so much more. But the greatest privilege for me is to get to know people and to travel alongside them on their journey through life, with all its ups and downs, twists and turns. I find this incredibly motivating and believe that the powerhouse of prayer and faith help me on this journey. And although I am far from perfect, I know that with God's help I can continue to try to make a difference. It may be a struggle at times, but perhaps it is the struggle that makes the difference!

Over the years I have been moved from one parish to another and, as you can imagine, this has taken its toll on me. That sense of loss when one leaves, of starting afresh all over again, has been a continuing pattern that I have lived with for a long time. But each parish I have moved to has been so enriching, and it has been such a privilege to journey with people in their joys and difficulties and to share in the cycle of their lives. I have been so fortunate to have shared in the joy of so many baptisms and weddings with families who have always welcomed me with much graciousness. But, of course, I have also had to face darker moments and have shared the hard times too, and sometimes they have been tough.

My life as a priest has been greatly blessed by God, but also by the presence of so many wonderful people. When I returned home from Rome, I valued the opportunity to catch up with my family, which made me feel healed and renewed. I still feel the same way whenever I visit my family, especially my father, who is ninety-five years old.

At this point, I would like to give a flavour of my twenty-one years of parish life.

St Matthew's Parish, Ballymacarett, 1992

It was about five thirty p.m. on Hallowe'en and I remember receiving a call from the local police station to say that there had been a shooting. I had only been in the parish about two months. My brother was staying with me and he drove me to Beechfield Street. I dashed down the street to the pub where the shooting had taken place.

Everyone was gathered outside in a panic, many still wearing their Hallowe'en masks – it all seemed so macabre. I rushed up the stairs and remember feeling a sense of evil hanging in the air. I composed myself as best I could, then anointed the victim and gave him absolution, while the paramedics continued to do their work. They worked so hard and I admired their courage – I can still hear that man breathing in and out, in and out, his head bandaged like a mummy, all these years on.

I remember going to pieces afterwards, astonished that someone could treat a fellow human being with such hate. It was a shattering experience for me and it led me to question my faith. And yet I put my trust in God, for it was His call that had brought me into that situation. My parish priest, Father E. O'Brien, was extremely supportive.

This was my first – though sadly not my last – experience of coming face to face with the raw reality of the Troubles.

Rome, 1991–2

I was sent back to Rome in 1991 to complete my extra studies in Moral Theology, and during that year my colleagues and I took turns to celebrate Mass in some of the local convents. When my turn came, we were due to celebrate Mass in the convent of San Gregorio Magno, whose sisters had close links with the Irish College. It was very early in the morning and as I approached the convent, scarcely awake, I noticed quite a number of cars at the gates, which struck me as unusual. When I ventured into the sacristy, I was told that Mother Teresa was there.

Well, despite my surprise, I went ahead with the celebration, and during Mass I noticed a small figure deep in prayer at the back of the oratory. I had the privilege of giving Mother Teresa Holy Communion, and after Mass she wanted to meet us. She seemed to have a bad cold when she came into the sacristy, but I remember looking at her eyes and thinking how youthful they were. She asked us to pray that she would be able to open more places in other countries to look after the poor. Her spiritual energy and enthusiasm were spellbinding and this was one meeting I would never forget.

Diocesan Adviser, 1990–91, 1994–2006

I was a regular visitor to the schools in the Diocese, which is the second largest in Ireland. I had trained to be a teacher, and the classroom was my natural habitat. Here I encountered faith and hope, and watched the seeds of faith develop, as the teachers encouraged the children to grow and prepared them for the challenges of life that lay ahead. My responsibility in those years was to give advice and to develop programmes that would help in the delivery of Religious Education. Since music formed a central core for me, I felt that I could build bridges with the children through music and use it as a means to encourage a sense of inner hope and belief. It is vital that children have a positive experience of faith to sustain them in the years to come. I found that children's clutter-free minds were open to the possibility of stillness and self-belief, even though many came to school with so much baggage. I remember moments of sudden insight, of gems coming out of the mouths of babes, when things simply made sense. I wanted these children to experience hope before they became too conscious of the worries of the world. I was greatly enriched by all the children I encountered on this journey, as I hope they were too.

Cushendun Parish, 2006–9

Cushendun will always be a special place for me, as it was my first post as a parish priest. It was here that I began to get to grips with parish life, while a major restoration programme of the 209-year-old church began. This period of my life was blessed with the support of many wonderful people, and there

Celebrating Mass in Knocknacarry Hall, Cushendun, during the restoration of St Patrick's Cathedral, Craigagh, 2009.

was a real buzz as we all pulled together to achieve our goals. This was also the time when our singing together as The Priests began to take off, and there was a sense of excitement in the air and of embarking on a journey. I appreciated the care and kindness of all the people in my parish and I will never forget them.

I was extremely sad to move on from Cushendun in 2009, while our restoration project was still ongoing; it was undoubtedly one of the most painful times of my life as, once again, the dark clouds thickened and I was faced with another change. However, I was soon to discover that the outlook was not all dark! My new parish of Newtownards and Comber made me feel so welcome, and no sooner did I arrive than I was caught up in finalizing the restoration of the Church of Our Lady of the Visitation, built in 1872. I was bringing to completion work that had been the vision of the previous parish priest, helped by the great team he had around him. The church was reopened on 20 June 2010, and what a joy it was to be part of this great celebration.

10 February 2004

This date is forever etched in my mind. A phone message reached me while I was in a Primary 3 classroom to say that my mother had collapsed. I managed to get through to my brother, who told me that she had died.

It was a devastating day. The drive home was so difficult and the tears were relentless. The loss seemed unbearable and it overwhelmed me. And so, lost in this sea of emotion, we buried our mother. Everyone I met reminded me of a time or an experience associated with Mum – happy days, happy memories that touched us all and reinforced just how special she was. As many people know, the shock waves of bereavement are incredible and the ripple effect of such deep-seated emotion can take you by surprise, and for me, it is still felt today. In a sense, music has come to our rescue once more; our mother always encouraged us in this endeavour and now I feel it has helped to heal the pain of her loss. We were recently in Derry for the summer concerts, and it was wonderful to dedicate the evenings to our mother and to all those who have supported us. She watches over us in many ways, thank God.

Cycles of Life

The ebb and flow of life rushes in and out
Upon the shores of our lives, of that there is no doubt.
Woven patterns of love and loss are all there to be seen
Revealing golden threads of the eternal, all redeemed.

Father Martin

5

Meditations

If we pray, we will believe;
If we believe, we will love;
If we love, we will serve.

Mother Teresa

Father Eugene

MANY PEOPLE HAVE ASKED HOW we manage to keep going in the midst of what has undoubtedly been, for the past two years at least, a very busy schedule. We have to keep up with parish and diocesan responsibilities and remain up to date with what's happening around us, while at the same time being available, sometimes at very short notice, for TV or radio interviews, while not forgetting to Tweet on our Twitter site and update the website. It is all very daunting. Where do I go or what do I do to recharge my batteries?

Friendship

Over the last twenty-five years of my life as a priest I have learned much about myself, the priesthood, and the gifts I have been given, as well as about my many shortcomings, and

I have become increasingly aware that although acquaintances may be many, friends are few. As we go through life we don't stop making friends, but it's undoubtedly a much slower process in our middle and later years than in adolescence or early adulthood. Maybe we tend to trust less in people as we grow older, which is a real pity.

Despite this, in the past two years I have made new and lasting friendships, although based on a different kind of dynamic than in the past. For starters, through music and being part of The Priests, I have met people from all over the world whom I would not otherwise have had the chance or pleasure to meet. A few have become real friends: people whom I can confide in and who will be honest enough to tell me the truth about myself, saying what I need to hear rather than what I might want to hear. That's one of the values of friendship. My batteries are recharged through contact with my friends new and old: by calling to see them, being part of their family lives, eating with them, going to concerts with them, enjoying their company, emailing them and so on. That's what friendship is all about – being at one's ease in another's company and not having to be on one's guard or on edge, or anxious about how one is perceived.

Art

Works of art are a constant source of inspiration. There's nothing I like more than going to a museum or art gallery simply to enjoy the works of all kinds of artists, both famous and not so famous. Art is more than mere colours on a canvas, just as music is more than notes on a stave. Art, like music, is truly timeless. What was painted perhaps hundreds of years ago continues to communicate across the years to the viewer today. It still has something to convey and speaks for all times and all seasons.

One of my most enduring memories of studying for the priesthood in Rome is the opportunity I had to follow the progress of the experts who cleaned the famous Michelangelo frescos in the Vatican's Sistine Chapel, the private chapel of the Pope and the place where his successor is usually elected by the College of Cardinals. I remember well the controversy the cleaning process caused among some experts, who thought it would inevitably damage the frescos. I'm no expert in art conservation or restoration, but I do recall my amazement as the covers were removed from the restored parts of the Sistine ceiling. You could see very clearly the contrast between the frescos dulled by years of candle smoke and not-so-expert restoration in the past, and the fresh, vibrant colours now revealed. We were now seeing the frescos as Michelangelo had painted them. Experiences like that are to be treasured.

Art has also helped me through grief and bereavement.

Several years ago, not long after I had been appointed to my present parish in Ballyclare and Ballygowan, and in the wake of a series of deaths and funerals, my own mother's included, I just needed something to revive me, to rekindle hope and joy at a time of intense sadness and grief. After a series of funeral liturgies in the parish, I felt the need to be uplifted by some happy experience. So, able to clear the diary for a few days, I chose to return to Rome, a city I love, with its art galleries and public spaces, in the hope of being refreshed by the timeless beauty of sculpture, painting and architecture. It was just what I needed and it did the trick. Rome, some say, is an open-air museum. It was a tonic just walking through the city, wandering along street after street, stumbling upon a small piazza never visited before, encountering the buzz of ordinary people going about their everyday business of buying and selling flowers and vegetables in the Campo dei Fiori or other equally beautiful parts of the city.

Most of us aren't lucky enough, of course, to live close to a museum or to have daily access to works of art that can inspire us. Whenever I need a cultural fix, the internet can come in handy. Instead of having to travel to far-away places to see works of art face to face, I can summon them in seconds at the click of a button. How marvellous that is! Through the wonder of technology we have access to a world of information, culture and science, which can be of such benefit and inspiration to us all.

The Sunday Sermon

The Sunday sermon presents a constant weekly challenge. It is, of course, not an optional extra to the Sunday service, but an integral part of the celebration of the Lord's day, and, ideally, requires careful preparation. In my experience, people are very tolerant of their priest or minister, who might not be the world's best preacher. However, people do rightly complain if sermons are too long, boring, unconnected with everyday life, too erudite, too simple or, at worst, irrelevant. Those of us who are required to preach can probably recognize all those criticisms and apply them to ourselves from time to time.

I do not claim to be the world's best preacher – God forbid – but my parishioners do tell me when they have enjoyed a sermon, and, indeed, when they have not. In the latter case, I must admit it's usually when I haven't given sufficient thought to the readings of the day and their relevance to many of my parishioners. In the former case, it may be the happy result of having mulled over the readings for a few days, done some background reading about the context of the Scriptures, then grappled with a theme that might be easily highlighted for my parish community. Finally, there's the spontaneity of the moment . . . but that's under the exclusive control of the Holy

Spirit and not me. When these elements collide, the results can be marvellous, even memorable.

Being aware of local and wider issues that can affect a community or congregation is also part and parcel of preaching a good sermon. During my years of preparation for ordination, a very wise and highly entertaining Professor of Sacred Eloquence (what a wonderful title!) from Maynooth, the national seminary of Ireland, reminded us that Karl Barth, the great evangelical theologian and preacher, had advised that to preach effectively one had to have 'the Scriptures in one hand and the newspaper in the other'. So a sermon, if it is to strike a chord, should, ideally, be relevant to a person's life.

That all sounds very simple and reasonable, but it still remains a weekly challenge to put all the ingredients for a successful sermon into the mixing bowl and produce a substantial dish that can feed the souls of both the young and the not so young. It is not an easy matter, especially if one depends solely on one's own abilities. On the other hand, there's always the inspiration of the Holy Spirit, or the accidental but no less inspirational off-the-cuff remark that can provide the focus for a whole sermon in just a few words. I can't say this happens to me every Sunday, but it does from time to time, much to the relief, I'm sure, of my listeners.

Difficult Issues and Prayer

From time to time, certain issues arise that can be difficult to deal with, involving a person or a group of people in the parish or in the context of Church life outside the parish. How do I approach such problems?

On one hand, I am the local priest in charge of a particular parish, with a commitment to the community entrusted to my pastoral care. I am known personally to all my flock and, because my parish is small, I have the advantage of knowing most of my parishioners. That's a huge advantage when it comes to dealing with sensitive issues and can go a long way to helping to resolve problems that crop up from time to time.

On the other hand, however well known I may be to my parishioners as a priest I am clearly identified with the huge international body that we call the institutional Church, with all its rules and regulations, its traditions, its doctrines and ethical principles. At the local level, those traditions and principles are strong, but they are increasingly challenged by significant numbers of people who, for one reason or another, decide to reject the institutional Church and its teachings in favour of something more personal and more suited to their individual lifestyles. People are generally wary of institutions of any sort, and the modern dynamic that exists between the individual and the institutional Church means that traditional values and views are not only questioned more openly than they would have been in the past but are more easily rejected. No doubt these tensions have always been there, but in a world where people are better educated than ever before and are able to articulate their opinions and criticisms, and where, let's be honest, the representatives of the Church have, from time to time, let people down or destroyed people's trust, it is little wonder that some people experience a crisis of faith. If they are lucky, people can look to their priest for direction at such a time. But this is not always the case, of course, and this can be a source of great sadness.

During my twenty years of work in the Marriage Tribunal, I have come into contact with several individuals who have felt extremely angry that an estranged spouse is seeking an annulment of their marriage. Their reaction is a very natural one, especially where children are involved. I have also had to speak with those hoping to obtain an annulment after a long and involved tribunal investigation has not met with success. Meeting people in these difficult situations has taught me to understand and accept the raw edge of people's emotions at significant times in their lives. In such circumstances, the Psalms and the Scriptures are always a rich source of inspiration for me. Personal prayer is also a great help in times of difficulty, helping me to renew my trust in God, who is always there even if we feel alone. Jesus did this when he was worried and afraid, and when he too felt abandoned in the Garden of Gethsemane; he turned to prayer.

Here are some of my favourite short prayers:

The Nunc Dimittis / The Canticle of Simeon

At last, all powerful Master
You give leave to your servant
To go in peace, according to your promise.
For my eyes have seen your salvation
Which you have prepared for all nations,
The light to enlighten the Gentiles
And give glory to Israel, your people.

Extract from Night Prayer of the Church

Save us Lord while we are awake
Protect us while we sleep
That we may keep watch with Christ
And rest with him in peace.

The Anima Christi

Soul of Christ, sanctify me
Body of Christ, save me
Blood of Christ, inebriate me
Water from Christ's side, wash me

Passion of Christ, strengthen me

O good Jesus, hear me

Within Thy wounds hide me

Suffer me not to be separated from Thee

From the malicious enemy defend me

In the hour of my death call me

And bid me come unto Thee

That I may praise Thee with Thy saints

and with Thy angels

For ever and ever

Amen

Prayer for Trust in Jesus

O Christ Jesus,
when all is darkness
and we feel our weakness and helplessness,
give us the sense of Your presence,
Your love, and Your strength.
Help us to have perfect trust
in Your protecting love
and strengthening power,
so that nothing may frighten or worry us,
for, living close to You,
we shall see Your hand,
Your purpose, Your will through all things.

St Ignatius of Loyola

Hail Mary full of Grace. Father Eugene praying at the shrine of Our Lady of Graces, Ballyclare.

Music and Food

When I was a student at Queen's University, Belfast and still ignorant about music, a very dear priest friend, Eamonn McDevitt, introduced me to the simple joy of listening to music. He had a considerable collection of vinyl LP records, which he played on a simple mono record player. He later upgraded to stereo, much to our delight! During the summer holidays we would be invited to his parochial house to listen to music and have supper . . . yes, he was also a great cook.

Food and music go together so easily, and I happily combine the two as often as possible. Following Eamonn's example, I try, whenever I can, to gather a few friends around the kitchen table to experience my latest cooking triumph (or disaster!) and for some chat, serious or light-hearted. Those gatherings, and others when someone else is the host and I am one of the guests, are always enjoyable, even if we do eat a little too much! But, as another dear friend of mine always says in such circumstances, 'excess is part of every celebration!'

So, what culinary delights can I assemble in the kitchen? Well, there's my definitive tiramisu, which is always a real favourite with my guests. Other regulars include spaghetti carbonara (which must have just the right amounts of egg, double cream and Parmesan cheese), penne arrabiata (which must be fiery and piquant), and lasagne. One of my mother's favourites was insalata caprese – that colourful mix of tomatoes, mozzarella cheese, basil leaves and just the right amount of virgin olive oil and balsamic vinegar for a dressing . . . it's hard to beat. Risotto is another favourite; even though it takes a bit of time, the rewards are always worth it in the end.

Most importantly, enjoying food is all about sharing – about community and giving. Throughout history, and certainly in the Bible, food has played its part in bringing people together; when we break bread with one another, we are of course sharing and giving sustenance, we are celebrating all manner of events, including life and death. So, although I love to practise my culinary skills, I am also aware that in sharing my table with others, I share part of me and who I am.

The Priests in Concert

In the past two years, we have sung in more places than I would ever have thought possible: London's Albert Hall and Apollo Theatre, Sydney's Music Centre, New York, Toronto, Montreal, Dublin, and various cities on our recent UK and Ireland concert tour.

Every concert performance brings its own share of nerves and tension. It's never easy to cope with nerves before a concert and each of us has a different way of preparing for a performance. Years ago I would have been so nervous that I wouldn't have eaten all day. The prospect of a concert in the evening would have left me on tenterhooks for the whole day. But with age and experience, my preparation routine has changed. I now have a good meal two hours before a concert, which provides me with the necessary stamina, although ideally the meal should not contain cream and I should not eat too much. If I were to sing on an empty stomach, I would literally feel a gap in the pit of my stomach, and I like to feel that I have a reservoir of strength for the vocal demands that lie ahead.

A less sinister version of Men in Black! Enjoying some downtime in Sydney after singing in St Mary's Cathedral, where The Priests were presented with a Platinum Disc for their first album.

While I make sure that I have sufficient energy for what is a very physically demanding experience, I also make sure that I have enough space and time in my pre-concert routine to prepare psychologically too. This involves psyching myself up for the concert earlier in the day or even a few days beforehand, going over the lyrics and the music, and making sure I know which songs each of us will be introducing and what to say by way of introduction. I am much better at being spontaneous than having a rigid text I feel I must stick to. Nevertheless, I must have a few ideas in my head about a song if I am to do it justice by way of introduction. A period of quiet before a concert is a real must for me, just to help me focus. And then finally, Martin, David and I have a few moments together when we say a short prayer, asking God, who has given us the gift of singing and the love of music, to grant us the grace and opportunity to sing to the very best of our ability and to bring the joy of music to all those who will be in the audience that evening. After that, it's all systems go!

This small insight into our preparations will, I hope, give a clue as to how much music and performance mean to us all. We feel blessed, because music not only has the power to lift our spirits and inspire us, but it feeds our souls. It is also our gift to others.

Father Martin

Wellsprings

In life we all need the wellsprings of inspiration, from which to draw hope in order to move ahead. These wellsprings can come in various forms, whether they be people, books, places or more besides.

There are many demands made on the life of a priest, but it is important to remember that the person fulfilling this vocation is only human, with a need to set limits. I try to ensure that my spirit is supported and well nourished, so as to avoid fatigue and stress.

We rely on God to support us, and I believe that He sends us little moments of inspiration. It's important to be aware of and open to these special moments, to see them and appreciate them, for inspiration breathes new energy into life's experiences. Throughout life I have experienced a wide range of varying emotions, including loss, pain, rejection, joy, belonging, hope, happiness and peace – but I can reflect back and know that they are all instrinsic parts of the rich mosaic of life.

In terms of my own inspiration, one essential element is that I need a place where I can be completely at ease – where I feel at home and at peace. This place, my own space where I live, is where I keep objects that remind me of my life's journey, and where I can really let my hair down and be myself. Here I can pray or reflect, wind down and take stock of my day. Being able to metaphorically unravel the everyday events that I face and make sense of all that has occurred is vitally important to me.

But I don't need the bricks and mortar of my house to feel that I am at home. Certain places are very important to me too. For example, I love the Glens of Antrim because they hold many dear memories. Being there in that beautiful place, being able to walk on the beach, allows me to think of the ebb and flow of life, the storms I sometimes have to face and negotiate, with the help of God.

Places evoke memory, encourage a sense of stillness – they can help to clear the mind and allow you to see things anew. Visiting places of natural beauty – whether standing at a high point in Glenarriffe Forest Park, or viewing the rugged beauty of Glenshane Pass, or the pristine sands of Donegal or Glenveagh – can refresh your soul. I would at times stop off at a little place near Dungiven on my way home. I would walk down the pathway past the standing stone and recall the legend of Finvola, princess of the O'Cahan clan; eventually I would reach the ruins of an old Augustinian monastery. Here I would sit and savour the silence, thinking of a time when God was the central focus for the monks of the monastery. This serene place would settle me and enable me to find that still point. Another place that is special for me is the little church of St Brecan, nestled in the trees of St Columb's Park. It is another quiet touchstone of faith and peace which gives me the space I need for reflection and prayer. Sustained by places such as these, which hold so many memories, I return to my duties refreshed and more disciplined, more able to give of my time to those I serve. New possibilities for prayer are also open to me.

Travel, too, adds new dimensions and new experiences

which can be revisited in our minds through the years. All my travel experiences have brought me face to face with other cultures, and these experiences lap against the shores of my own life, enriching it all the more. I thank God for these moments.

Reflections at a cross in Craigagh Cemetery, Cushendun, 2009.

In my experience, people have often been a real source of hope. People of steadfast faith – be they parents, grandparents, parishioners, or even children – have shown me how they have overcome great adversity. Through them, I have come to realize that struggling to overcome problems can lead to new growth and greater strength. In the course of my duties, I have been called out to all sorts of situations, and have shared many experiences with my parishioners that have resulted in great moments of inspiration. I also remember my teachers, whom I have spoken of in earlier chapters, and how, together with my parents, they inspired me to reach for new horizons. My teachers were people of great faith, and their sense of conviction was enormously motivating. I remember that they always had time to listen to me, to share the moment with me. People such as this shape us, don't they?

The saints can be so influential. St Francis of Assisi went against the trends of his day and provided refreshing evidence of faith in the God of love. I really appreciate his caring nature, for he shows us how important it is to care for each other in this world – to look out for and protect one another. I am also inspired by St Ignatius of Loyola, the founder of the Jesuits, whose sense of determination as a youthful soldier spurred him on to found a religious order. When things get me down and I am at a low ebb, his prayer provides a real wellspring of support for me, giving me hope and the strength to continue.

> Lord Jesus Christ, take all my freedom, my memory, my understanding, and my will. All that I have and cherish, you have given to me. Now I return it all to be guided by your will. Your grace and your love are wealth enough for me. Give me these, Lord Jesus, and I ask for nothing more.
>
> *St Ignatius of Loyola*

The Irish saints also inspire me, with their sense of engagement with the world, and their quest to bring faith from their shores to central Europe, as St Kilian did, who went to Wurzburg in Germany and whose tomb I have visited, and St Columbanus from Bangor in Northern Ireland, who is now buried in Bobbio in Italy. Whatever motivated these people, I feel that God was certainly at the centre of their lives.

Places of pilgrimage, such as the Holy Land, undoubtedly bring us in touch with Christ, and journeying to them can spur us on in our own journey of faith. I remember going to Skellig Michael, off the coast of Kerry, the last outpost in the west of Ireland before America. This ancient site was spectacular, especially in the blaze of sunshine that accompanied my visit, the tiny individual cells still perfectly intact. It was as if the monks had gone off for the day. Such austerity, such utter dedication to keeping their faith and culture alive, even when they were attacked by the Vikings – why? A weatherbeaten cross stands there proudly, reminding me of the need to remain true, despite our brokenness, to the way of Christ. When I was in Rome, I would stand at the tomb of St Peter or one of the many other saints, to remind me of the need to let the love of God in and to abandon myself all the more to their influence. Somehow their stories are interwoven with my own experiences as I struggle on.

Friends

Good friends are so important; they enable us to discover more about ourselves and they bring out the best in us. Sometimes there can be rough patches – rapids, as I call them! Perhaps the rhythm might change in a relationship, but that is OK too. For friendship is a gift we can all be enriched by, a place where our shortcomings are forgiven. The skills we employ in friendship are also essential in our relationship with God: sharing, talking, listening, giving advice, love, care and more. I have many good friends who are a great support to me, and their presence in my life has been enriching. They have been there for me in times of isolation, joy, crisis and loneliness, and I deeply appreciate this. Taking time out together, sharing a problem, or just being there for someone is so life-giving. I thank God for my friends and pray that as we continue our journey together, our relationship will continue to grow.

One man, Father Frank O'Farrell, who is now deceased, was a great source of inspiration to me, and to all the students at the Irish College in Rome. 'Never make a decision when you are down,' he would often say. This piece of advice has stood me in good stead for many years and has been a huge support to others too.

The Written Word

Ever since I was very young, I have found great inspiration in books. I recall reading *Irish Short Stories* as a child, as well as *The Lamb*, a story about reaping the harvest, and *The Awakening*, in which the son of a fisherman comes to the realization that he wants to be a fisherman like his father, a book that gives an insight into vocation, a real epiphany.

Poetry, too, has been a constant source of comfort and insight, and has led me to many moments of reflection. Poetry energizes me, and helps me to make sense of our fragmented world. I am inspired by wonderful, thought-provoking writers such as Shakespeare and Seamus Heaney, and Brian Friel has given me great pleasure. The Psalms are beautiful too – I especially love Psalm 139, because it celebrates life and the wonder of who we are. I enjoy dabbling in poetry myself, for it helps me to make sense of my experiences, using words as a tool with which to paint my ups and downs. I don't mind admitting that I also love good detective novels, by authors such as Agatha Christie, or television serials. Intricate plots and exotic settings can lift your spirits and take you out of your everyday world. Human nature unfolds before us through the wonderful characters portrayed on the page or on screen.

Art

I love art. It has always spoken volumes to me. I enjoy a little pilgrimage around art galleries, where I can forget about myself and delve into the artists' minds. I remember visiting the Hermitage in what was then Leningrad, now St Petersburg, at the age of eighteen and feasting my eyes on the works of Rembrandt, Monet, Poussin, Canaletto, Leonardo da Vinci, Tiepolo and more. This visit to Russia made a deep impression on me, and I journeyed especially to see one painting. My first sighting of it was behind a half-open door, but it was instantly recognizable: *The Prodigal Son* by Rembrandt. This is a painting I revisit often in my thoughts, for it depicts the son kneeling before his forgiving father. The son has lost all dignity, everything; all he has is the dagger he carries. He is rough, unshaven, dirty and barefoot. The portrayal of this intimate encounter is incredible, for the painting draws you to the two figures and engages you in their drama. How I would love to step into the picture and talk with the Prodigal Son and his father – who stands serenely in front of his son, his hands resting gently on his son's shoulders as if trying to release the burden he carries. Through the father, God's tenderness is tangible, reminding us of the parable's message that we are forgiven by a just and caring God.

Caravaggio is an artist who also fascinates me, despite his rather shady history. Here is a man whose gift of art brought people off the streets to be immortalized on canvas. I did not encounter this great artist's work until I became a student at the Irish College in Rome, and I am so grateful that I discovered him. Caravaggio plays with light and darkness in his paintings, and they are full of drama and anxiety, perhaps revealing the light and shade of his own tempestuous life.

These great and gifted artists have refreshed me and helped me to regain a sense of perspective on life. Sometimes I take out my art books in the evening and simply gaze at what I see before me, like a child full of wonder at what I behold. These great works have helped me through the difficulties and challenges of faith, and engaging with the paintings in this way is like a form of prayer. Art helps me when I am down and inspires me in both joyful and difficult times. Thank God for all these experiences.

Icons, too, are an intimate and moving source of inspiration, each telling its own story (icons are said to be 'written', not painted) and inviting you to share the experience. I am constantly amazed at the stunning iconography of the Orthodox Church. I was recently given an icon by Sister Aloysius McVeigh, a great friend of my mother's, now sadly passed on. I met her at an art gallery in Pump Street in Derry, which had just completed an exhibition of her icons. In her eighties, here was a woman of undoubting faith, a living icon. She showed me an icon of St Patrick, so different from the usual portrayal of the saint. 'We have to get back to the real Patrick,' she said. She invited me for tea and after some prayer she showed me the icons she had written. I was so touched; each icon was like a child that had been invested with all that she was. This encounter brought me in touch with a living example of faith and belief: what a privilege.

Music

When I get really tired and stressed out, music reenergizes me. Soft, quiet music soothes my spirit, and can provide a calming backdrop to my day. Sometimes a piece of music makes me stop in my tracks: Delius's 'The Walk to the Paradise Garden', 'Ladies in Lavender', 'Le Onde' by Ludovico Einaudi, 'The

Armed Man' by Karl Jenkins, 'The Lark Ascending' by Vaughan Williams and Debussy's 'La Mer' – these and many more envoke a sense of tranquillity and fire my imagination. Music is indeed the language of the soul. Sometimes I sing, just to enter into the heart of a piece, and I get lost, caught up in the sentiments, the story.

Music and art have been major mediums of prayer and hope across the centuries, so why should it be any different today? Music is like a landscape to be traversed, and provides a route to tranquillity and peace by soothing and easing the human spirit. I find the musicians' stories inspiring too, and the context and circumstances in which they wrote their music. A Gregorian chant can also calm and soothe me, and prevent me from being distracted and caught up in the Martha syndrome! You may recall how, in the Bible, Martha lives with her sister, Mary. When Jesus visits their home, Mary sits at their Lord's feet, listening intently to what he has to say. Martha, on the other hand, busies herself with preparations for his visit. When she complains about being left to do all the work, the Lord reminds her that 'you are worried and upset about many things, but only one thing is needed. Mary has chosen what is better.' (Luke 10: 38-42)

Reliving experiences through music is also a great way of calling to mind happy times, as music is a major portal to the world of memory. Through music I can step into another world and be immersed in wonderful, nourishing sounds. I can unravel and forget my inner struggles, freeing myself to refocus and reenergize myself in preparation for what lies ahead. I recommend this as a way of escaping, even momentarily, from the stresses and strains of life. As Purcell said, 'Music, music for a while shall all your cares beguile.'

My musical tastes are quite catholic and I enjoy a lot of contemporary music. In the past few years, Father David, Father Eugene and I have all enjoyed meeting many people in the music industry – such as The Killers – and I have been impressed by these encounters. Getting to know new artists and becoming familiar with their music and their lyrics has been an enormous privilege, and has opened up my mind to many new possibilities.

It is important to nurture yourself sometimes, in order to prevent yourself becoming overwhelmed by the pressures of duty and service. The irony is that in order to serve others better, we should also serve ourselves. The stronger we are, the more energy we will have for those around us. It is a lesson that is easy to forget! I always remember the adage of St Bernard of Clairvaux, who said, 'Do not spend yourself so much on others that you forget about yourself.' As a priest, I am confronted on a daily basis by life situations that are both difficult and joyful. Spanning this spectrum can feel a little like riding a rollercoaster. In just one day I can experience so many different emotions that at times it can be quite draining, and I am grateful for the support of friends, family and my parishioners.

So far, I have mentioned all the aspects of my life that give me comfort, support and inspiration, and I hope that this will offer you some insight into the gifts that surround us, and all there is in this world that we can share and enjoy. We all need sources of support and hope, of sustenance and care. Sometimes I am only too aware of my brokenness and this can cast a long, dark shadow over my life. But with God's love and His help, I continue to trust, to learn, to be open to change, to abandon the shadowlands of life – even though it is a daily struggle, a daily renewal of commitment.

In the hustle and bustle of my life, I enjoy moments of solitude. Alone at home, I draw inspiration from silence, which helps me regain a sense of enthusiasm. This is the positive side of being alone. The other side of the coin is, of course, loneliness – something which, I am sure, we all experience at some point in our lives. Loneliness eats into the human soul; it is a place that is uncomfortable, unwelcome. When I feel lonely, I need more support from those around me, to enable me to journey through the barren impasse and move out into new, more fertile territory beyond.

To conclude, there are wellsprings in all our lives, but we need to have the courage and the sensitivity to be open to them. Perhaps we need others to divine those wellsprings, but when they are discovered, life changes. In life there can be challenges, and sometimes we have to be true to ourselves in the midst of them. Realizing one's limitations can be painful, but it brings a real sense of freedom. Learning from the past, from decisions made and journeys completed, also adds to what life can give. Self-belief and self-esteem are needed today more than ever before, to meet the pressures of modern life, but we are not alone in this task. We need to return again and again to our wellsprings, to divine that which gives us life. None of us is an island; we are all inextricably linked – that is what it means to be human.

Wellsprings

Deep within the richness resides
Waiting to be unpacked, besides
It offers us a life line true
Which constantly renews, renews.

Father Martin O'Hagan,
'Feast of the Transfiguration'

One prayer that has been a constant source of inspiration is the prayer of St Basil of Caesarea, which I use often on hospital visits or when I am out visiting the sick of the parish:

Steer the ship of my life, good Lord, to your quiet harbour,
where I can be safe from the storms of sin and conflict.

Show me the course I should take. Renew in me the gift of discernment, so that I can always see the right direction in which I should go. And give me the courage to choose the right course, even when the sea is rough and the waves are high, knowing that through enduring the hardship and danger we shall find comfort and peace.

Father David

Were you to enquire of me, 'Where do you find your inspiration? Where do you look for support and help in your life? Where and to whom do you go for help when you need it?' I would have to answer that there is no one single, identifiable source. Rather there is a multiplicity of wells from which I draw life-giving water, these being principally faith, family and friends, prayer, priesthood and parishioners, music and the natural world. It is from sources such as these that I draw my deepest nourishment and sustenance. These are the wells that I visit regularly, spending time first at one and then at another, visiting them all in turn, depending on the nature and extent of my thirst.

The most profound of these wells of refreshment, the one whose waters I find most intensely life-giving, is the well of faith. My relationship with God has been like a constant, unbroken stream running through the ever-changing landscape of my life. It has been there since my childhood days in the 1960s while I was growing up in Ballymena in the heart of my family, where I learned the basic truths of the faith at the feet of my parents, and all through my schooldays in the 1970s when my faith was oh so dramatically awakened. It was then that God became my overwhelming passion and the direction of my life seemed so clear.

In the intervening years, it's not so much that my faith has been constant; it hasn't. On the contrary, the strength of my faith, if anything, has appeared to wax and wane in seemingly equal measure, like a radio signal that fades in and out, sometimes strong and sometimes faint.

Yes, there are wonderful and wondrous times when faith carries me along like a mighty river in full flood, rushing and tumbling and leaving me drenched and high, exhilarated and gasping. At other times, as I have perceived it, my faith has dwindled away to the merest trickle, providing barely enough to refresh the parched soul and appearing, alarmingly, in danger of drying up. And then, without warning, the stream of faith dives to some obscure, subterranean, subconscious place so that I am no longer aware of its presence. For a time I feel arid, rootless, and fear that I have irrevocably and irretrievably lost my way, until at some unexpected moment faith resurfaces to quench anew the parched soul and remind me – 'oh, ye of little faith' – that while I may be inconstant, God is never so. It is the God of my faith who is constant and it is to that privileged relationship that I inevitably turn and return in good times and in bad, but never, it seems, more fervently and earnestly than in times of need.

As I draw closer to the fiftieth milestone of my life – at this point still several years off – I can easily recall the prayers of my childhood which my mother taught my brother, sisters and me. Each morning, before sending us out to school, she would gather us around her at the foot of the stairs. After helping us to bless ourselves with the sign of the cross in that exaggerated, enthusiastic way that children do, she would lead us in prayer, saying, 'Good morning dear Jesus, good morning God's mummy. God bless Daddy and Mummy, Fiona, Frank, David, Nicola, Paula and Philippa.'

And then a little child's voice would innocently pipe up, 'And Dixie!' (the cat) and someone else would add anxiously, 'And don't forget Rusty!' (the dog).

It's probably just as well that we never had a tank of goldfish.

And we would go on in our sing-song voices, 'God bless

everyone in Nana's house and Granny's house. God bless Auntie Enda.'

Enda is my mother's sister, who is a religious sister of the Congregation of St Louis, the same religious order to which Gertie, our beloved music teacher, also belonged.

'Thank you, dear Jesus, for making Fiona's legs better.'

My sister Fiona was born with a dislocated hip and spent long periods of her childhood in hospital, where she endured many operations. Amazingly she later became an inspirational PE teacher and, thank God, has lived a fully active life up to now, never allowing herself to be limited by a continuing and frequently debilitating condition. As children we understood it was Jesus who had answered our prayers and made her better.

And we would continue with our prayers, saying:

Infant Jesus meek and mild,
look on me a little child.
Pity mine and pity me
and suffer me to come to Thee.
Heart of Jesus, I adore Thee,
Heart of Mary, I implore thee,
Heart of Joseph, pure and just,
in these three hearts I put my trust.

The Holy Family theme would continue with:

Jesus, Mary and Joseph, I give you my heart and my soul.

Jesus, Mary and Joseph, assist me in my last agony.

Jesus, Mary and Joseph, may I breathe forth my soul in peace with you.

Amen.

I wasn't quite sure what 'my last agony' meant and I certainly didn't like the sound of it, but I figured, whatever it was, it was obviously a good thing to have Jesus, Mary and Joseph on my side to help me. I still believe that.

Such prayers as these and many others that were taught to me in my childhood have sustained me and served me well through the years, even into adulthood, particularly on the many occasions when inspiration has been lacking. I am deeply indebted to my parents for the faith that they passed on to me. And indeed, that indebtedness extends also to my grand-parents, James and Eileen Delargy and Mary and Robert McMullan, who were all people of deep faith and who were an inspiration and example to their own children and grandchildren.

So, it is fair to say that the foundations of my faith were already firmly in place by the time I found myself at St McNissi's College. Singing for Mass in the college choir under the leadership of wee Sister Gertie helped to consolidate my faith further. As well as singing the old favourites, like 'How Great Thou Art' and 'Be Thou My Vision', she also introduced us to some of the classic choral motets, such as Mozart's 'Ave Verum Corpus' and Palestrina's 'O Bone Jesu'. Benediction each Saturday evening was part of our timetable of liturgical prayer and very quickly we became familiar with the 'Tantum Ergo' and other Gregorian chants. Even African rhythms and harmonies were part of our choral repertoire – we once performed extracts from the Congolese Missa Luba Mass for a radio broadcast. It was wonderful to be performing pieces such as these, not merely for the sake of artistic performance, but as an expression of personal and communal worship in a living and spiritually dynamic liturgy. As a result of these experiences, a clear understanding was formed in my mind of the vital relationship between music and singing and faith.

My enjoyment of music and singing would be a crucial factor in the profound awakening of my faith that occurred during my teenage years, and which was to set and seal the direction towards priesthood that my life would subsequently take.

Father Aidan Kerr, my Latin teacher, used to lead a small prayer meeting for a group of his students each week. At that time it wasn't generally known to the student body that this prayer meeting was going on. I suppose it was kept discreet so that the boys taking part in it would be spared the merciless teasing that was often a feature of life in our all-boys school.

Occasionally in the evenings I would hear the muffled sound of distant voices filtering down the corridor to the room I shared with my older brother, Frank. Somewhere in the building there was a group of boys singing hymns! Who on earth could be singing hymns at this time of the evening and where was the sound coming from? I wanted to be where they were. I wanted to be part of it, to be part of the singing. I had to find out. At the age of thirteen, joining a prayer group was not on my list of '100 things to do before you die'. But the music, and singing – that was another matter, and for the sake of that, I was keen to give it a go.

Thus came about my introduction to a new way of praying; not the kind where one would recite by heart the familiar prayers of one's childhood, or read someone else's learned prayers from the pages of a beautifully bound book. No, this was a more personal kind of prayer, the kind that arose from the heart as much as from the mind, which engaged the imagination as much as the senses, the body as well as the voice. And the songs we sang were not the formalized ones we sang in choir. They were modern, contemporary, up to date – with themes that both spoke clearly to a young person's heart and expressed what was in a young person's heart; they were the kind of songs a young person could relate to.

And how we sang! We sang about how God would never

forget us, His people. He loved us even more than a mother loved her child. He loved us so much that He had carved our names on the palm of His hand. He would never forget us or leave us orphans, for we were His own.

The effect of this new prayer experience over the course of the rest of that year was to awaken in me the desire to know God in a more personal way. If God existed, as I believed He did, then, according to my thinking, it would not be good enough for Him to be distant, remote or hidden. Infinitely better would be a personal God who would be at least as interested as I was in being involved in a meaningful relationship. It was not enough for me to know intellectually that God is all good, all loving and all powerful. No, I needed to encounter Him personally, to know Him, to experience His love, to see and feel His power. And I wasn't willing to wait until the hereafter to experience that. God, I believed, could and should reveal Himself to me now. It didn't seem an unreasonable expectation; after all, it wasn't as if I was asking for a major miracle – just a small sign, enough to let me know He was there, that He could hear me. Many times I heard how Jesus said, 'Whoever asks will receive. Whoever seeks will find and the one who knocks will always have the door opened unto him,' and I was prepared to take him at his word. And, boy, did he answer my prayer!

Even now, it is difficult to find the right words to express the manner in which God answered my prayer. To give an inadequate account of such an intensely personal experience, one that I think of as my treasure, my pearl of great price, would be to run the risk of that profound experience appearing trivial or superficial. It's a risk, however, that I am willing to take.

It happened one afternoon as I was in the college chapel by myself, praying. By that time I had grown into the habit of going to the chapel each day by myself to spend some time in prayer. (Call me odd if you like – I probably was a bit odd!) This day was different though. After a period of silent meditation, I began to sense that I was connected with God in a way I had never been before. The sensation was almost physical. I felt as if I were being filled from the inside with the love of God. The love grew and increased within me to the point where I felt I could no longer contain it and that if it continued I would surely burst. It was not my love for God, but rather God's love for me. It felt like a gift. I could do nothing about it other than wait and be filled. Looking back, I can well appreciate how St Peter on the Mount of the Transfiguration could say with the fullest enthusiasm, 'Lord, it is wonderful for us to be here,' for it was as if that day God had given me a glimpse of His glory and, yes, it was truly wonderful. The predominant feeling was of joy – profound, intense, overwhelming, indescribable joy. My heart could not contain it all. Saint Peter refers to this kind of joy in his first letter when he says,

You do not see him, yet you love him; and still without seeing him, you are already filled with a joy so glorious that it cannot be described, because you believe.'

1 Peter, 1:8

I have since come to understand this joy as one of the 'fruits' or effects of the Holy Spirit. Saint Paul speaks of these in his letter to the Galatians 5:22. That joy remained with me for some considerable time. I was on fire. I had a fire burning within me that refused to go out. It was as if I had been granted my own personal Pentecost, for I could not prevent myself from going out and gabbling to anyone who would listen about God's amazing love. Not for a millisecond did it occur to me to stop and think about what I was doing or how it would be received. I understood intuitively that this gift had not been given to me for my own private benefit. It had been given to me for others. God's love was meant not only for me. It was for everyone. People needed to know about it and by giving me such a precious gift God had also laid upon me the duty and responsibility of being his evangelist. I was drunk on the Spirit and I would forgive anyone who during those days found themselves on the receiving end of my excited gushing and concluded that I was a mad, emotional freak.

The intense feelings of love and joy have long since subsided, a fact that I have on occasions regretted, although perhaps it is just as well for such feelings would have been impossible to bear, and I too would be unbearable. In any case, one is not meant to remain forever on the mountain top. There is also the road to Calvary to be followed and the taking up of one's cross to be endured. That's part of the journey too. But the memory of that privileged experience and the indelible mark it left on my soul have sustained me through all my life and, it must be said, through many dark days and painful times. For ever since that time in the thirteenth year of my life I have known, in a way that for me is utterly beyond contradiction, that God is very near, and that he loves me as His son.

My name is David. It means 'Beloved of the Lord'. I was well named. And if you want to know who I am, then I will tell you . . . I am a beloved son of God, and that is the truest thing about me.

I soon came to the realization that not every prayer experience would be like that one. It is impossible to re-create that wonderful experience by one's own efforts and, indeed, it might be self-serving to try. Nevertheless, I have since found that the most meaningful prayer experiences have often been those where I have gone into my private room and prayed to my heavenly Father who is in that secret place. One of my favourite Scripture texts for meditation is the following passage from Matthew's Gospel 11:28, where Jesus says to his disciples:

Come to me all who labour and are overburdened
and I will give you rest.

Shoulder my yoke and learn from me
for I am gentle and humble of heart
and you will find rest for your souls.
Yes, my yoke is easy and my burden light.

I frequently use this text for meditation before the Blessed Sacrament. There are times when I feel burdened with worries and anxieties of my own. I may be worried about a family member who is ill or about a situation that has arisen in the parish that I'm not sure how best to handle. Sometimes a misunderstanding arises between me and a parishioner or I experience opposition or criticism on account of an unpopular decision I have made. I am not unaffected by these. Sometimes I am burdened down by the weight of my own sins, my own failures, and a sense of my own inadequacy. It's difficult sometimes to be an earthen vessel with the responsibility of carrying such an infinitely precious treasure. I feel burdened at times by other people's expectations of me, by the Church's expectations. While I usually try to put my best foot forward, to present my best self to the world, I know that the reality at times is somewhat less worthy, less noble, and I fear that my poverty may be evident, to my shame.

The past few years have been intensely difficult ones for all of us in Ireland and elsewhere who esteem the Church and once held her officials in unquestioningly high regard. I have felt at times the acute pain and sense of injustice of the abused as well as the bewilderment, confusion and disillusionment of the faithful. I have also felt, at times, the pressure and the pain of those who are judged harshly in the court of public opinion and condemned for their failings. I feel burdened sometimes because I don't always know how to respond to the anger expressed by so many, and which I feel myself just as keenly.

And it is at such times that I hear Christ say to my soul, 'Come to me all you who labour and are overburdened and I will give you rest.' So I come to him in the Blessed Sacrament seeking relief and refreshment, and rather than relieving me of my burdens I hear him say, 'Take my yoke upon your shoulders.'

I do not come from a farming family, at least not in the last couple of generations, and, in any case, farming methods have changed considerably since the time of Christ, so the significance of a yoke was initially beyond me. I needed to remind myself what a yoke is and how it works.

A yoke is a shaped wooden beam that is placed across the shoulders of an ox that is being harnessed to a heavy load, for example a plough or a heavy cart. The purpose of the yoke is not to lay on an additional burden. On the contrary, its effect is to help spread the weight evenly so that the load may be more easily borne. Sometimes a yoke is attached to the shoulders of two oxen, enabling them to share the load.

When Christ asks me to take his yoke on my shoulders, he

is offering to help share my burden. 'A burden shared is a burden halved,' and the load that was once weighing so heavily now becomes bearable. And so I often imagine yoking myself to Christ in such a way that we are joined one to another under a double yoke, the two of us moving side by side, bearing and sharing the burden together. I am no longer alone. Christ walks beside me. He is with me in this situation. He is by my side, not just as my Saviour and my Lord, but more usually as a co-worker in the vineyard, a compassionate companion, a wise friend. And the burden does indeed become light.

Of course, there is more to accepting the Lord's yoke than simply allowing him to share and thus lighten my burdens. It also means that I must go where the Lord leads me, to walk where he walks, to go where he wants me to go. It also requires of me that I learn from his humility and his meekness. These are difficult lessons and I confess that I still have quite some way to go in assimilating them.

Sometimes I imagine that Christ is seated by my side or opposite me, an invisible presence, but no less real for all that, and we talk. When I stand at the altar offering the Mass, sometimes he stands at my shoulder or just behind me. I sense him there, taking an interest in all that I do and say in this sanctifying, saving work of his that he has entrusted to me. I sense his hand on my shoulder, a reassuring touch, gently reminding me that I am not alone, that he is there, that it's not about me. It's about him.

Christ once said to his disciples, 'I am with you always, to the end of time.' This promise applies not only to the Church but also to the individual believer.

There is a beautiful ancient Gaelic prayer which reflects just such a strong sense of the presence of Christ. It is attributed to St Patrick, who during his long years of captivity developed a very strong sense of Christ's immanence. It is known as 'The Breastplate of St Patrick'. This was a favoured prayer of the late Cardinal Tomas O Fiach. I remember once seeing him during Mass in St Patrick's Cathedral in Armagh; he came back to the altar after distributing communion to the faithful and I heard him say this prayer with an energetic conviction while vigorously purifying the sacred vessels.

Christ with me, Christ before me, Christ behind me,
Christ in me, Christ beneath me, Christ above me,
Christ on my right, Christ on my left,
Christ when I lie down, Christ when I sit down, Christ
    when I arise,
Christ in the heart of every man who thinks of me,
Christ in the mouth of everyone who speaks of me,
Christ in every eye that sees me,
Christ in every ear that hears me.

Theologians tell us that in the administration of the sacraments the priest acts *'in persona Christi'* – in the person of

Christ. This refers to the existential union that is created between a priest and Christ by the sacrament of ordination. The effect of this is that when the priest speaks and acts in the sacraments, he is not acting and speaking in order to represent himself, but in order to represent Christ. It is the priest who says the words and performs the actions, but it is Christ himself who acts. The priest is merely the unworthy agent through whom Christ speaks and reaches out to his people.

I consider how it can sometimes be that a blind person can rely on a sighted person to be his eyes, a deaf person can rely on another person's ears for his hearing, and a speaking person can be the voice of one who is voiceless. In the celebration of Mass, whether I am proclaiming the Gospel or standing at the altar offering the sacrifice, I consider how at that moment I am Christ's eyes to see, his ears to hear, his voice to proclaim and praise. I am his hands to take, to bless, to break and give the Bread of Life. A poor substitute, I know, but what an awesome privilege to be a priest, to act 'in persona Christi'.

St Teresa of Avila, the sixteenth-century Spanish mystic and Carmelite nun, had a clear sense of how this can also be applied, in a broader sense, to all the faithful – and she expressed this idea with beautiful simplicity in this prayer:

Lord Christ,
You have no body on earth but ours,
No hands but ours,
No feet but ours.

Ours are the eyes through which your compassion must
    look out on the world.
Ours are the feet by which you may still go about doing good.
Ours are the hands with which you bless people now.

Bless our minds and bodies,
that we may be a blessing to others.

Father David standing amidst the remains of his church, St James, Aldergrove,
after an arson attack, July 1998.

As I look back on the words that I have just written, there is a beautiful psalm that comes to mind which I think expresses very well what I have been trying to say. It is a modern take on Psalm 105, and I share it with you in the hope that it may resonate with you too.

How great is my God,
and how I love to sing His praises!
Whereas I am often frightened
when I think about the future,
and confused and disturbed
by the rapidly changing events about me,
my heart is secure and made glad
when I remember how He has cared for me
throughout the past.

When I was brought forth from my mother's womb,
God's hand was upon me.
Through parents and people who cared,
He loved and sheltered me
and set me upon His course for my life.
Through illness and accident
my God has sustained me.
Around pitfalls and precipices
He has safely led me.
When I became rebellious

and struck out on my own,

He waited patiently for me to return.

When I fell on my face in weakness and failure,

He gently set me on my feet again.

He did not always prevent me from hurting myself,

but He took me back to heal my wounds.

Even out of the broken pieces of my defeats

He created a vessel of beauty and usefulness.

Through trial and errors, failures and successes,

my God has cared for me.

From infancy to adulthood

He has never let me go.

His love has held me – or followed me –

through the valleys of sorrow

and the highlands of joy,

through times of want

and years of abundance.

He has bridged impassable rivers

and moved impossible mountains.

Sometimes through me,

sometimes in spite of me,

He seeks to accomplish His purposes in my life.

He has kept me through the stormy past;

He will secure and guide me

through the perilous future.

I need never be afraid,
no matter how uncertain
the months or years ahead of me.
How great is my God,
And how I love to sing his praises.

Psalm 105, from Psalms/Now
by Leslie Brandt and Corita Kent

I realize that in this short essay I have focused my reflections on the role that music, faith and prayer have played in providing me with inspiration and support, and have said little about the other wellsprings that have also played a crucial role, namely my family, friends and parishioners, whose understanding and patience have carried me and affirmed me on so many occasions.

I have been on the receiving end of so much generosity and kindness in my home and in the places and parishes I have served. I know I am being supported daily by the prayers of my parents, and so many others besides, and for that I am truly grateful. It is to my family, to my friends, to those who have been my companions at various stages of my journey thus far, and to you who will read this book that I dedicate this beautiful prayer:

To God Who Sings Through Us

God who sings in our hearts, as the flute needs openness to receive the breath of melody, we pray to be open to the many ways that your symphony of love plays in our lives. Thank you for the ways that your enlivening Spirit touches us and moves through our beings. Remind us often that each one of us is a special instrument of yours. Come and make music through our lives. Dance through our days and sing in our hearts.

Breathe through us, Music Maker, and let your song weave a melody through all we are and do. May we acknowledge your power at work in us and open ourselves to this blessing.

Out of the Ordinary *by Joyce Rupp*

Postscript

Reflections on Our Unexpected Musical Journey

Dear Reader

It was a little over two years ago when Martin took a call from a man called Liam Bradley. Liam was looking for a priest who could sing the Latin Mass for a project that Sony Music were planning and had heard that the O'Hagan brothers sang. He wondered if it would be possible to meet up, so Martin immediately called us both and we arranged to meet Liam at the Good Shepherd Centre. After some deliberations we agreed to record a couple of songs together, and one or two on our own. The recordings seemed to go well, but as busy priests we didn't have time to give much thought to the recording session, and carried on with our lives and our parish duties.

Two days later, Liam called again with the news that Sony

Music wanted to offer us a worldwide record deal, and we suddenly realized that our busy lives could soon become a whole lot busier!

The next few days and weeks were a blur. We spent some time trying to take it all in and thought endlessly about the potential consequences. There just seemed to be so many questions that needed answers. For example, we were, first and foremost, parish priests with many responsibilities. How would we manage to balance these with life as recording artists? We assumed that we would make an album, but exactly *how* did you do that? We thought that perhaps we'd have one or two songs played on a classical radio station and then we'd return to our 'day jobs'. We recalled how the late Pope John Paul II had told people to 'go out into the deep'; these words resonated with us and gave us much encouragement. So although we had no idea what to expect and it all seemed a little daunting, we accepted Sony's offer of a record deal. From that moment it was all systems go!

In April 2008, we signed the much-reported Sony contract in front of Westminster Cathedral and that night the story featured on the ITV news. We hadn't told anyone we knew, not even our families, and yet there we were, large as life on national television!

By the end of the year, we'd recorded our debut album with a huge orchestra at the legendary Windmill Lane Studios, and travelled extensively to promote our album. From Spain to the USA, from London and Canada to Australia – it was a whirlwind of activity. We broke a Guinness record for the fastest-selling debut classical album in the UK, appeared in *Time Magazine* and on numerous television shows around the world, including *The Late Late Show* in Dublin and *Tonight with Jonathan Ross* for the BBC. We sang for the President of Ireland, Her Majesty the Queen, Prince Charles and the Duchess of Cornwall, and chalked up unexpected record sales and positions in some of the world's most prominent Top 10 charts. We were even nominated for two Classical Brit Awards.

We have also been fortunate enough to play in front of live audiences in venues of all shapes and sizes – a rare treat that is hard to put into words. Performing with a talented group of musicians, to living, breathing people who have made the effort to come to see and hear you, is very special and an enormous privilege. There is a wonderful sense of anticipation when one travels to a show and prepares for a performance. As the orchestra stirs into action and you step out on stage, you feel the heat of the lights, hear the applause that greets and envelops you, and all at once you are carried away to a musical world where you are able to leave any troubles, trials or tribulations at the door. It's quite overwhelming, completely uplifting and something we never tire of. A total joy for us, and, we hope, for our audiences too.

It never entered our minds that something so wonderful and unexpected could happen, when we were hardly in the first flush of youth! But it has been and continues to be a fascinating, demanding and challenging adventure. And if you were to ask us if we would do it all again if we knew what was involved, the answer would have to be a resounding YES – and for very good reasons. Our unexpected journey has given us the chance not only to meet many wonderful people, but to share our love of music with audiences around the world, and we are eager to find out what might be around the next corner.

We owe a great deal to those of you who have travelled with us on our epic journey and welcome those of you who are new to our story. We wish you all a safe and happy year, and despite these challenging economic times, we thank God for the good things that we *do* have.

God Bless,

Father Eugene, Father Martin and Father David

Acknowledgements

We would like to thank the many people who have accompanied us in *Soul Song*, and in particular our parishioners, past and present, parish staff and secretaries, the staff at the Good Shepherd Centre, fellow Catholic and Protestant clergy, regional marriage tribunal colleagues and staff, Marie O'Sullivan, Sister Mary Jo Corcoran, Finola McCool, Clare Cody, Fionnuala Jay O'Boyle, Elizabeth Bicker, Daniel O'Neill, Ruth McGinley, Fergus Shiel, Roisin and Andrew McCarroll, Maureen and Billy Shannon, the Trowlen family, Hugh Heffron and family, Nuala Murray, Rose Rogan, members of the Performers' Club, Castleward Opera, Lyric Opera, Cappella Caeciliana and the many Music Societies with whom we have enjoyed singing, Sam Wright and Ian Brown, Liam Bradley and the team at Bright Artist Management, Enda Walsh and the Amberville Recording Studios team, the Sony Music team, Nick Raphael, Mike Hedges, Ger McDonnell,

Sally Herbert, Haydn Bendall, Olli Cunningham, Ciaran Byrne, John McLaughlin, David Thomas, Lisa Davies Promotions, Steve Schofield, Hardwick and Morris, Martin Deller at Northrop, McNoughton and Deller, the team at Transworld Publishers, including our editor Brenda Kimber, Eoin McHugh, Katrina Whone, Kate Samano and Madeline Toy, our fans, website and live concert followers, and all our friends who, with love and support, have helped us on our journey.

The Priests praying together at the Good Shepherd Church, Belfast.

Moments of Stillness

Sister Stanislaus Kennedy

In her long-awaited new book, Sister Stan draws upon her memories of childhood and the special moments of awareness and mystery which have nourished and enriched her life.

As she offers simple reflections to help us focus on the many gifts and blessings that surround us each day, she helps us to connect to our inner world, and the deep, nurturing silence that lies within.

The Road Home
My Journey

Sister Stanislaus Kennedy
Foreword by President Mary McAleese

In this inspiring memoir, social innovator and political activist, Sister Stanislaus Kennedy, or Sister Stan as she is affectionately known, looks back on her early life in rural Ireland, and to the life-changing decision she made at the age of eighteen to become a nun.

Inspired by the work of Mary Aikenhead, who founded the Congregation of the Religious Sisters of Charity in 1815, and her mentor, Bishop Peter Birch, she helped to set up a comprehensive model of community care in Kilkenny that was to become a blueprint for the rest of Ireland.

Reflecting on the many challenges she has met, we see how Stan has worked tirelessly – sometimes against strong opposition – to help establish vital voluntary groups, such as Focus Ireland, now the biggest national organization for the homeless; Young Social Innovators, and the Immigrant Council of Ireland. She also created The Sanctuary Meditation Centre, a place of peace and healing which is located in the heart of Dublin's bustling city centre.

Inspiring and thought-provoking, this fascinating memoir provides a unique insight into the life and work of one of the most influential social activists of our day. It is, quite simply, the remarkable story of a remarkable woman.

Benedictus
A Book of Blessings

John O'Donohue

'We have fallen out of belonging. Consequently, when we stand before crucial thresholds in our lives, we have no rituals to protect, encourage and guide us as we cross over into the unknown. For such crossings, we need to find new words. What is nearest to the heart is often farthest from the word. This book is an attempt to reach into that tenuous territory of change that we must cross . . .'

In sharing words of profound grace and wisdom, master storyteller John O'Donohue's *Benedictus* offers blessings to shelter us as we confront the many challenges we face on our journey through life.

Living in an anxious world – a world so often dominated by unwelcome change, unhappiness and even despair – many readers will find comfort in John O'Donohue's illuminating introductions, covering areas such as Beginnings, Desires, States of the Heart, Callings and Beyond Endings, and the blessings themselves provide an inspiring and reassuring new vision of possibility. It is also a vision of hope and belonging for this sometimes troubled world.

Anam Cara
Spiritual Wisdom from the Celtic World
John O'Donohue

When St Patrick came to Ireland in the 5th century AD, he encountered the Celtic people and a flourishing spiritual tradition that had already existed for thousands of years. He also discovered that where the Christians worshipped one God, the Celts had many and found divinity all around them: in the rivers, hills, sea and sky. The ancient Celtic reverence for the spirit in all things survives today – a vibrant legacy of mystical wisdom that is unique in the Western world.

Now, in this exquisite book, Irish poet and scholar John O'Donohue shares with us the secrets of this ancient world. Using authentic Irish prayers and blessings, he reveals the treasures that lie hidden within your own soul and the 'secret divinity' in your relationships. As he traces the cycles of life and nature, he draws from the holy waters of Ireland's spiritual heritage to lead you to a place where your heart can be healed and nourished. It is a place where you will discover your own anam cara, your true 'soul friend'.

Echoes of Memory

John O'Donohue

In this powerful, evocative poetry collection, master storyteller John O'Donohue explores themes of love and loss, beginnings and endings. Inspired by the ancient wisdom of the Celtic tradition and the rugged, majestic landscape of his birth, the west of Ireland, here he also creates a unique vision of a place and time, and the echo of a memory that will never fade.

The Four Elements
Reflections on Nature
John O'Donohue

Air * Water * Fire * Stone

In *The Four Elements*, poet and philosopher John O'Donohue draws upon his Celtic heritage and the love of his native landscape, the west of Ireland, to weave together a tapestry of beautifully evoked images of nature.

As John explores a range of themes relating to the way we live our lives today, he reveals how the energy and rhythm of the natural world – its innocence and creativity, its power and splendour – hold profound lessons for us all.

With a foreword written by his beloved brother Pat, this illuminating and thought-provoking treasury is a unique collection of reflections inspired by the ancient wisdom of this earth.

Eternal Echoes

John O'Donohue

There is a divine restlessness in the human heart today, an eternal echo of longing that lives deep within us and never lets us settle for what we have or where we are. Now, in this exquisitely crafted, inspirational book, John O'Donohue explores that most basic of human desires – the desire to belong. It is a desire that constantly draws us towards new possibilities of self-discovery, friendship and creativity.

In *Eternal Echoes* John O'Donohue embarks upon a journey of discovery into the heart of our post-modern world – a hungry, homeless world that suffers from a deep sense of isolation and fragmentation. With the thousand-year-old shelter of divine belonging now shattered, we seem to have lost our way in this magical, wondrous universe.

Here, as we explore perennial themes and gain insight from a range of ancient beliefs, we draw inspiration from Ireland's rich spiritual heritage of Celtic thought and imagination. It is a heritage of profound, mystical wisdom that will open pathways to peace and contentment, and lead us to live with creativity, honour and compassion the one life that has been given to us. Destined to become a timeless classic of vision and hope, this is an imaginative tour de force by one of today's most inspirational writers.